INSIGHT GUIDES

AUSTRALIA

POCKET GUIDE

Map Included

⊙ Walking Eye App

YOUR FREE EBOOK AVAILABLE THROUGH THE WALKING EYE APP

Your guide now includes a free eBook to your chosen destination,
for the same great price as before. Simply download the Walking Eye
App from the App Store or Google Play to access your free eBook.

HOW THE WALKING EYE APP WORKS

Through the Walking Eye App, you can purchase a range of eBooks and destination
content. However, when you buy this book, you can download the corresponding
eBook for free. Just see below in the grey panel where to find your free content and
then scan the QR code at the bottom of this page.

Destinations: Download essential destination
content featuring recommended sights and
attractions, restaurants, hotels and an A–Z of
practical information, all available for purchase.

Ships: Interested in ship reviews? Find independent reviews of river and ocean ships in this
section, all available for purchase.

eBooks: You can download your free accom-
panying digital version of this guide here. You
will also find a whole range of other eBooks,
all available for purchase.

Free access to travel-related blog articles
about different destinations, updated on a
daily basis.

HOW THE EBOOKS WORK

The eBooks are provided in EPUB file format. Please note that you will need an eBook reader installed on your device to open the file. Many devices come with this as standard, but you may still need to install one manually from Google Play.

The eBook content is identical to the content in the printed guide.

HOW TO DOWNLOAD THE WALKING EYE APP

1. Download the Walking Eye App from the App Store or Google Play.
2. Open the app and select the scanning function from the main menu.
3. Scan the QR code on this page – you will then be asked a security question to verify ownership of the book.
4. Once this has been verified, you will see your eBook in the purchased ebook section, where you will be able to download it.

Other destination apps and eBooks are available for purchase separately or are free with the purchase of the Insight Guide book.

TOP 10 ATTRACTIONS

THE BLUE MOUNTAINS
This dramatic area of forested ravines and pristine bush is just west of Sydney. See page 63.

KAKADU NATIONAL PARK
Home to giant termite mounds and ancient Aboriginal art. See page 109.

BAROSSA VALLEY
Australia's best-known wine-growing region is located in South Australia. See page 153.

GREAT BARRIER REEF
Located off the Queensland coast, this is one of the natural wonders of the world. See page 90.

SYDNEY
Home to Australia's most iconic architecture. See page 40.

ULURU
Also known as Ayers Rock, this enormous sandstone monolith has been venerated by the local Aboriginal peoples for centuries. See page 117.

PERTH
A stylish and vibrant modern metropolis. See page 127.

UNIQUE WILDLIFE
Encounter kangaroos, koalas, wombats and crocodiles in their natural habitat. See page 12.

GREAT OCEAN ROAD
This coastal drive offers some truly spectacular views. See page 179.

MELBOURNE
An elegant and sophisticated city. See page 161.

A PERFECT TOUR

Day 1–3

Hello Sydney

Say good morning to Australia, taking breakfast overlooking sparkling Sydney Harbour (see page 40), and spend at least two days soaking up the city from several angles. Explore history in the Rocks, climb the iconic Harbour Bridge and catch a show at the Opera House. Pick a sunny day to catch a ferry across the harbour to Manly. Graze at a seafront restaurant or learn to surf with the experts.

Days 6–7

Melbourne

A long day's drive or a short flight from brash Sydney will take you to Australia's sophisticated southern capital, Melbourne (see page 161). Multi-layered Melbourne's skyscrapers conceal a labyrinth of bluestone alleys that host fashionable boutiques, hipster cafes, and a riot of street art. Galleries, theatres, nightclubs and sporting extravaganzas gild this entertainment and culture hub.

Days 4–5

Blue Mountains

It's a short drive or train journey to see the Blue Mountains (see page 63), to the west of Sydney. Here you can be as active (canyoning, abseiling and bushwalking) or as inactive (mountain vistas and gourmet meals) as you like.

Day 8

Phillip Island

Your best chance of seeing a penguin without heading towa[rds] Antarctica is on a day tour from Melbourne [to] Phillip Island (see pag[e] 175), where you can also spot koalas and f[ur] seals.

OF **AUSTRALIA**

Days 12–14

...p End

...re a car in Darwin to explore the best of the Northern ...rritory's Top End (see page 104). Catch sight of the ...mping crocodiles of the Adelaide River and plunge ...to crystal clear pools in Litchfield National Park. For ...cultural insight like no other, take an Aboriginal bush-...cker tour in Kakadu National Park.

...ays 9–11

...airns

...ropical Cairns
...ee page 90) is a
...ur-hour flight and a
...imate zone away from
...elbourne. Hop aboard
...fast catamaran to
...e Great Barrier Reef
...nd spend a day diving
...r snorkelling. For a
...fferent viewpoint on
...ay two, zip through
...opical rainforest
...n a cable car up to
...uranda for a lunch of
...opical fruit.

Days 19–21

Queensland

Southern Queensland, blessed with perfect weather, offers awesome activities in a playground of adorable beaches and rainforests. Brisbane (see page 80) is a vibrant gateway to the glitzy Gold Coast, where surfing and theme parks keep the adrenaline flowing.

Days 15–18

Red Centre

From Alice Springs (see page 113), take a day tour to the West MacDonnell Range before moving on to Yulara, five hours' drive from Alice, to experience the shifting hues of Uluru and Kata Tjuta.

CONTENTS

⬤ INTRODUCTION_____10

🏛 A BRIEF HISTORY_____22

📖 WHERE TO GO_____39

New South Wales_____40
Sydney 40, Excursions from Sydney 63, Going West 63, Heading
north 65, The Hunter 66, Lord Howe Island 67, Heading south 68,
The Snowy Mountains 68, New South Wales outback 69

Canberra_____70
Designing the capital 71, City sights 73, North of the lake 74,
South of the Lake 75, Out of town 78

Queensland_____79
Brisbane 80, The Gold Coast 85, The Sunshine Coast 88, The Great
Barrier Reef 90, The Reef Islands 91, The tropical coast 98

Northern Territory_____103
Darwin 104, City sights 105, South and East of Darwin 108,
Kakadu National Park 109, Katherine Gorge 111,
Alice Springs 113, Uluru (Ayers Rock) 117, The Yulara
development 120, Surviving the outback 121, In case of
catastrophe 123

Western Australia_____124
Perth 127, To the coast 132, Fremantle 133, Rottnest Island 135,
Excursions inland 136, Natural wonders 138, The southwest 139,
The Goldfields 140, The Kimberley 142, Coastal attractions 144

South Australia_____145
Adelaide 146, Nearby places 151, Up the river 152, The Barossa
Valley 153, Kangaroo Island 154, Three peninsulas 156,
The Flinders Ranges 158, Coober Pedy 159

Victoria _____161
Melbourne 161, Excursions 173, Phillip Island 175, Wilsons
Promontory 176, The Goldfields 177, The Great Ocean Road 179

Tasmania _____181
Hobart 184, Excursions from Hobart 186, Port Arthur 187,
Launceston 189, Wilderness 190

😈 **WHAT TO DO** _____193

Sport _____193
Entertainment _____203
Shopping _____207

😋 **EATING OUT** _____215

⭕ **A–Z TRAVEL TIPS** _____224

🌐 **INDEX** _____250

🎯 **FEATURES**

The Commonwealth of Australia _____15
Brave but fallible _____28
Historical landmarks _____37
What's in a name? _____77
Perils of the deep – and the shallows _____95
From coast to coast _____126
Festival frenzy _____146
Why 'kangaroo'? _____155
It could have been Batmania _____162
Wiping out the Aborigines _____183
Australian champions _____202
Calendar of events _____213
Indigenous cuisine _____216

INTRODUCTION

Australia is a vast place. The country comprises almost an entire continent all by itself, sprawling over about 7.68 million sq km (2.97 million sq miles), making it about the same size as Europe. That's big enough to have several distinct climates – from cool temperate to tropical – and three time zones. The natural landscapes are correspondingly diverse, ranging from red deserts to green rainforests and from sandy beaches to snow-clad mountains. Epic natural beauty is complemented by sophisticated cities, where all the pleasures of urban life are at hand – usually with beaches and national parks on the doorstep.

AUSSIE STEREOTYPES

Perhaps because of its size and diversity, together with its isolation, Australia has been little known and even less understood for most of its history. A character in an Oscar Wilde play set in the Victorian era summed up the foreigner's blurred impression of Australia: 'It must be so pretty with all the dear little kangaroos flying about. Agatha has found it on the map.'

In many people's minds, the land down under still consists of vague images: the Sydney Opera House, Bondi beach, the Great Barrier Reef, the unforgiving Outback, and all those bizarre Australian animals. It's true that the kangaroo, the koala, the wombat, the platypus and the Tasmanian devil are unique to Australia, but there is much more to the country than this.

And what of the human population? Australians tend to be perceived as a laid-back

The open door

In 1922, the novelist D.H. Lawrence wrote: 'Australia is like an open door with the blue beyond. You just walk out of the world and into Australia.'

An Aussie bushman

bunch, fond of sunbathing, surfing and swilling cold beer. And there are the Australian 'types': a stockman herding sheep beneath eucalyptus trees, or a tanned bushman prospecting in the stark landscape of the Outback. Like most clichés, there's something to it. Statistically there is actually a sizeable obesity problem in Australia, but it remains very well hidden and most Aussies seem to relish the outdoor life. Many radiate health and either possess or admire tanned muscles. During the weekends, if they're not actually at the beach, they are usually playing sport, listening to football or cricket on the radio, or they're out in the garden barbecuing beef or seafood. To complete the picture, there's typically an icy beer at hand to pacify the fiercest thirst. Australians may not be the world's most insatiable beer drinkers, but they're in the premier league.

Prospectors seeking gold, opals or other minerals still roam the Outback, Australia's remote, sparsely inhabited backcountry. In the wild northern 'Top End', enormous crocodiles stalk unwary prey, sometimes coming a little too close to civilisation – about 100 are removed from Darwin's harbour every year. Remote cattle farms ('stations') are so big that stockmen conduct their roundups using helicopters. One of the stations is the size of Belgium.

However, these startling facts represent only part of the truth. Camping holidays or day-trips to national parks are as close as the overwhelming majority of Australians get to living in the bush. Australia is one of the world's most urbanised countries, with over 90 percent of its population living near the coast in the 10 biggest cities. More than one Australian in five resides in Sydney (population about 5 million). Melbourne is approaching the same size. Other state capitals – Brisbane, Adelaide and Perth – account for most of the rest of the population.

NATURAL WONDERS

For many people, Australia's natural wonders, its odd wildlife and its far-flung open spaces still eclipse everything else. The vast and starkly beautiful Outback holds an almost hypnotic appeal. When the best-selling author Stephen King took a short break from writing and roared into Australia's wide-open expanses on a motor-cycle, he described his sense of awe: 'If you stop, the silence is incredible. You feel very small; you can almost hear God breathing.' Bear in mind that you don't have to go as far as the Outback to find untouched nature. The Blue Mountains National Park, for example – a Unesco World Heritage Area – is only 90 minutes' drive from central Sydney.

Some extraordinary wildlife wanders the continent. Australia has a virtual monopoly on monotremes, mammals that lay eggs. Among them are the waddling, spine-covered echidna and the platypus, a half-aquatic furry mammal with a duck-like bill.

Rather more familiar are the continent's marsupials, equipped with pouches to solve the baby-sitting problem. Bounding across the landscape are numerous varieties of macropods ('big feet'), from small wallabies to giant red kangaroos. Another marsupial, the languid, furry koala, eschews violent exercise, spending its days

drowsing in the branches in a eucalyptus-induced haze. Its relative, the wombat – another vegetarian marsupial – prefers to burrow under stumps or logs, or in the banks of creeks. More commonly seen are possums, tree-dwelling marsupials that have colonised many suburban backyards, causing householders sleepless nights with their noisy nocturnal wanderings.

Birdwatchers here can count hundreds of species. Thrillingly colourful birds, such as the rainbow lorikeet, are as common as sparrows in other countries, and lyrical or humorous birdcalls provide a country music soundtrack every evening. These indigenous stars have names such as flowerpecker, honeyeater and kookaburra, but the favourite bird of crossword puzzlers – the emu – can't sing or fly.

Unsurprisingly, Australia has some unique specialities in the reptile department too, including 2-metre (6ft) goannas, exotic creatures like the frill-necked lizard and the bearded dragon, and the world's largest

Four wheeled drivers' heaven: the 'Big Red' dune in Queensland

Aboriginal child

crocodile, the salt-water croc, or 'saltie'. For good measure, the island contains more species of venomous snake than anywhere else on earth.

A CONTINENT CUT OFF

Australia has been isolated from other continents since it split from the remnants of the southern super-continent, Gondwana, about 40 million years ago. Cut off from the evolutionary mainstream, plants and animals developed in ways that have engrossed generations of scientists and astounded millions of ordinary tourists.

For millennia, the only humans sharing the continent with these animals were nomadic Aboriginal tribes. These first Australians are believed to have arrived from Asia, probably by boat, somewhere between 50,000 and 100,000 years ago. Australia's Aborigines lived within tribal boundaries they believed had been created by their ancestors in a period called the Dreamtime. Aborigines built no permanent structures but lived in a manner that ensured their survival in a harsh environment.

Their lives changed little until European explorers began arriving in the 17th and 18th centuries. The Dutch may have been the first to arrive, but the colonial history of Australia began properly in 1770, when Lieutenant James Cook landed on Australia's east coast and claimed all the territory he charted for King George III. Shortly after Cook's arrival, the British decided Australia was an ideal place to send convicts and in 1787, Britain dispatched a fleet of soldiers and convicts to colonise Australia, the farthest-flung point of its Empire.

In a relatively short time, the British Empire had casually seized the traditional lands of Australia's hunter-gatherers and Aboriginal peoples were dispersed and massacred. Australia's indigenous population (who now represent about three percent of the country's population) did not gain the vote until 1962 and were not included in Australia's official census until 1967.

The founding of modern Australia has left its mark on the national psyche, although the impact is fading. Australians were once notably defensive about their country, asking foreigners what they thought of it, then waiting anxiously for the answer. These days, Aussies are more relaxed about such matters. The descendants of convicts have long since been outnumbered by the descendants of free settlers, but if Australians can prove convict ancestry they do so eagerly – it's considered a mark of prestige.

☉ THE COMMONWEALTH OF AUSTRALIA

Since 1901, the six former British colonies of Australia have been an independent federal commonwealth with a British-style parliamentary system. Apart from the six states, there are also two territories, the Australian Capital Territory (ACT) and the Northern Territory. Australia's Head of State is Queen Elizabeth II. She is represented by a Governor-General, who is nominated by the federal government and appointed by the Queen. The Prime Minister heads the federal government and is the leader of the party that holds the most seats in the lower chamber, the House of Representatives. The upper house is the Senate. The federal parliament is based in Canberra, a city founded in 1913. Like Washington DC, in the US, Canberra lies in its own administrative zone, the ACT. Each state and territory has its own government and leader, called the premier (states) or chief minister (territories).

The country has much to be proud of. In little more than 200 years, a tiny European settlement founded in conditions of brutality, servitude and privation has prospered and transformed itself into a dynamic modern nation whose economy places it in the top 20 OECD countries in terms of gross domestic product. Tourism is one of the largest earners and a major employer, directly accounting for almost a million jobs, or almost eight percent of Australia's workforce.

Australia is a long way from its traditional northern-hemisphere allies: 9,720km (6,000 miles) from the US and 17,820km (11,000 miles) from Britain. But non-stop or one-stop flights make the going relatively easy. More distant in cultural terms are Australia's nearest neighbours, Indonesia and Papua New Guinea, a short flight to the north. The Asian connection is vitally important, however, both politically and economically. A look at the faces on any Australian city street shows the vastly increased flow of immigrants from South and Southeast Asia.

Since the early 1980s, cultural intermingling has revolutionised the national diet. Urban Australia now enjoys a collage of culinary influences with fresh, high-quality ingredients. All the state capitals have lively café scenes and at least one nearby wine-producing area, giving you the chance to sample wines at the cellar door. Climatic diversity allows Australia to produce both warm- and cool-climate wines and grow tropical fruit such as rambutans, custard apples,

Vines growing in the Hunter Valley

mangoes and lychees, as well as avocados, strawberries, blackberries, apples, pears, oranges and mandarins.

In the capital cities, you'll have no trouble finding restaurants serving excellently prepared cuisine from as far afield as Thailand, Mexico, Cambodia, Japan, France, Hungary, Spain, Lebanon, Turkey or Italy. In smaller towns, the choice is more limited, and you may have to settle for a meat pie, fish and chips or chop suey.

> ### Immigrant nation
>
> In Australia, four out of 10 people are immigrants or first-generation children of immigrants. Over 28 percent of residents were born overseas.

Australia's geographical superlatives are clear-cut. It is the world's biggest island. More accurately, it is the smallest and least populous (about 24.5 million inhabitants) of the continents, and the only one housing a single nation. Australia measures about 4,000km (2,500 miles) east to west and 3,200km (2,000 miles) north to south. It is 24 times the area of the British Isles.

The Great Dividing Range, stretching almost the entire length of the eastern continent, and with a maximum elevation of just over 2,000 metres (6,500ft), separates a narrow fertile strip on the coast from the Outback. West of the range, the country becomes increasingly flat and dry. Habitation becomes sparse and after thousands of kilometres the horizon is broken only by occasional mysterious protuberances including Uluru (Ayers Rock) and Kata Tjuta (the Olgas), and starkly beautiful mountains such as the Flinders and MacDonnell ranges. Then, in the far south of Western Australia, a repeat of the mountain range-coastal strip pattern heralds the Indian Ocean.

While Outback Australia includes regions of great natural beauty, much of the interior is arid, consisting of immense deserts and salt-pans. Only seven percent of the country is arable, which is why the settlement pattern has been so different from that of the US, and why the population is so much smaller. Non-arable land is not necessarily

Lush palm forest

unproductive: under the surface lie bauxite, coal, iron ore, copper, tin, silver, uranium, nickel, tungsten, lead, zinc, diamonds, natural gas and oil. Mining is one of Australia's biggest industries, accounting for about eight percent of the country's GDP.

A VARIETY OF VEGETATION

Australia is home to some of the world's best-preserved wilderness areas. Unesco's World Heritage List currently includes a total of 16 Australian regions, ranging from the Great Barrier Reef and the Tasmanian Wilderness to the Wet Tropics of Queensland and Uluru–Kata Tjuta.

The rainforests of Australia – healthy, vast and diverse – form one of the world's best-preserved wilderness areas. From the lush, dense jungles of tropical North Queensland, the rainforest region extends south to the planet's last great stand of temperate rainforest – the cool, moist forests of Tasmania. Apart from their sheer beauty, Australia's rainforests contain about half of all Australian plant species, including 'primitive' plant families providing direct links with the birth of flowering plants 100 million years ago.

At almost all Australian latitudes you'll see hardy trees of two main families. There are more than 600 species of flowering acacia (including the golden wattle from which Australia derives its national colours) and over 500 types of eucalyptus, ranging from low, stunted, scrub-like bushes to the great towering varieties of the highland forests. There are ghost gums, so-called because under the light of the moon they appear silvery-white, and rock-hard iron-barks, capable of blunting the toughest timber saws.

Australia is the world's flattest continent, although the nation's highest summit, Mt Kosciuszko (elevation 2,228 metres/7,308ft), is almost as high as Mexico City. You can ski in the Snowy Mountains of New South Wales from June to August/September. The country's first ski club, the Kiandra Pioneer Ski Club, was founded in 1870 – two years before the first clubs in the United States.

Australia is the driest inhabited continent, with only one river (the Murray) worthy of world ranking. The country's coastline is 36,735km (almost 23,000 miles) long and includes many sweeping beaches where you can wander for a whole day and see no one. You can dip a toe (or a surfboard) in legendary waters, among them the Coral Sea, the Timor Sea, the Pacific Ocean, the Indian Ocean and the Southern Ocean.

UNDERWATER WONDERS

Some of Australia's most colourful sights exist under the sea. Divers visit Australian waters to admire the sort of fish you see in a collector's tropical tank – only 10 times bigger. Gorgeous angelfish, clown anemone fish and moorish idols glide past the enthralled skin diver's mask. Big-mouthed sharks, sting rays and venomous scorpion fish may also be seen.

For enthusiasts of underwater spectacles, the most exciting place in the world is the Great Barrier Reef. This 1,944km (1,200-mile) miracle – a living structure of coral – thrills the imagination in its immensity and in the intricate detail of brightly hued organisms shaped like antlers, flowers, fans or brains. It's the world's largest living thing. The most sublime tropical fish congregate here, too.

The reef, one of Australia's top tourist destinations, has become ever more accessible with a choice of airport hubs, fast catamarans and permanent pontoons. Australia's developed air transport system puts the whole continent within reach: beaches and ski

The reef

The Great Barrier Reef is home to more than 1,500 species of fish as well as whales, dolphins, turtles and thousands of different crustaceans.

resorts, dynamic cities and Outback towns.

A LAID-BACK CULTURE

Even among such a wealth of natural wonders, it's the people you meet who often leave the deepest impression. Australians generally are a friendly, no-nonsense bunch – direct and to the point. 'G'day mate!' is a cheery greeting often heard, sometimes followed by 'How ya goin', alright?' Americans detect Cockney or Irish undertones in the Australian accent – yet some visitors from Britain or Ireland swear they can identify an American influence.

Many Australian terms are unique, as likely to baffle a Brit or American as a European. 'Don't come the raw prawn' is a picturesque example, fading now from general usage. It means 'Don't try to pull the wool over my eyes.' The happy-go-lucky expression 'She'll be right' has been largely supplanted by 'No worries, mate,' but they both mean the same thing – 'It will all be OK.'

The Aussie sense of humour can bewilder newcomers. It is peppered with ironic understatements and playful contradictions, such as: 'She's getting a bit warm' (as the shade temperature reaches 40°C or 104°F); 'You're not wrong, mate' (an expression of enthusiastic agreement); or 'Now there's a bloke who hates a drink' (meaning that the man is a heavy drinker).

Australians have a love of outdoor enjoyment and a passion for sport, from the home-grown football code 'Aussie Rules' and cricket to relatively new sports like baseball and basketball. The sunny climate has a lot to do with this, but so does the perception that the sporting field (or jogging track) is a place where social barriers are easily overcome.

Australia has a high proportion of migrants, and the nation's cultural mix is still evolving, but Britain and the US are still the main influences. British visitors often notice a California-style informality; American visitors are often surprised by the degree of Britishness remaining. At leisure, the majority of young Australians dress casually and watch American TV shows, but students at private schools continue to wear blazers and straw boaters like their counterparts in England. Cricket is played on local greens by teams sporting full whites, and on beaches and in backyards by bare-chested blokes in flip-flops.

Of course, ethnic and other rivalries do exist, and (given the country's history and cultural mix), visitors may witness some surprisingly xenophobic sentiments expressed – not least in the media and by politicians – but most Aussies fundamentally believe people should be given 'a fair go', and not be judged on preconceptions of class, race or gender.

Snorkeller with a whale shark, Ningaloo Reef, Western Australia

A BRIEF HISTORY

Australia has probably been populated for longer than Western Europe – possibly even twice as long. Humans first arrived from Asia at least 50,000 to 60,000 years ago, and some argue that it was far earlier. Professor Paul Tacon, an archaeologist at Griffith University, Queensland, claims that pollen core samples taken across Australia show changes in vegetation and deposition of charcoal 'beginning somewhere about 120,000 years ago'. He believes that these changes resulted from human activity.

The first migrations to Australia were most likely spurred by a period of glacial advance that encouraged the cave dwellers of the Northern Hemisphere to head for the sunbelt. This move set off a chain reaction, forcing more southerly folk out of their way. As ice caps accumulated, sea levels dropped drastically, meaning there were more land bridges, but it's thought the first people came via boat.

The first Australians had little difficulty adapting to the new environment. As Stone Age hunter-gatherers, they were accustomed to foraging, and the takings in the new continent were good: plenty of fish, berries, roots and marsupials to eat.

'The Dreamtime' is the all-purpose name for everything that came before. It puts Aboriginal history,

Traditional Aboriginal art depicts the Dreamtime

Aboriginal paintings, Kakadu National Park

traditions and culture under a single mythological roof. The Dreamtime's version of Genesis recounts how ancestral heroes created the stars, the earth and all the creatures. The Dreamtime explains why the animals and plants are the way they are, and how humans can live in harmony with nature.

NAVIGATORS ARRIVE

For millennia the Aborigines had Australia to themselves, but over the last few hundred years, the rest of the world has closed in. Like the search for El Dorado, everybody seemed to be looking for *Terra Australis Incognita*, the 'Unknown Land of the South'. Throughout the 16th century, explorers from Europe kept their eyes peeled for the legendary continent and its presumed riches. Some (including the Spanish, Portuguese and Chinese) may have come close, but the first known landing was by a Dutch captain, Willem Jansz, in 1606 while in search of trade outlets for *Oude Compagnie*. It was an anticlimax. 'There was no good to be done there,' was Jansz's conclusion as he weighed anchor.

'Beautiful lies'

According to the author Mark Twain, the history of Australia 'does not read like history but like the most beautiful lies... It is full of surprises, and adventures, and incongruities, and contradictions, and incredibilities; but they are all true; they all happened.'

The merchant adventurers of the Dutch East India Company were not to be discouraged, however. In 1642 the company dispatched one of its ace seafarers, Abel Tasman, to track down the elusive treasures of the farthest continent. On his first expedition, Tasman discovered an island that he called Van Diemen's Land – now known as Tasmania, after him. A couple of years later he was sent back. He covered much of the coast of northern Australia, but still found no gold, silver or spices. Like Jansz before him, Tasman had nothing good to say about the indigenous people, who impressed him as poor, hungry and unattractive brutes. The Dutch named Australia 'New Holland', but their reports on the land were so unpromising that they never bothered to claim it.

Another pessimistic view was reported by a colourful traveller, English buccaneer William Dampier, who had two good looks at the west coast of Australia towards the end of the 17th century. He found no drinking water, no fruit or vegetables and no riches. The local inhabitants, he wrote, were 'the miserablest people in the world'.

BOTANY BAY

Almost by accident, James Cook, the great British navigator, landed on the east coast of Australia in 1770 on a very roundabout trip back to England from Tahiti. Aboard his ship *Endeavour* were the skilled naturalists Joseph Banks and Daniel Solander. They found so many fascinating specimens that Cook was moved to name his landing place Botany Bay.

Cook claimed all the territory he charted for George III, coining the name New South Wales. He returned to London with glowing reports of a vast, sunny, fertile land, inhabited by a native people who were 'far more happier than we Europeans'.

In 1779, Joseph Banks, by now president of the Royal Society, came up with a novel idea. He proposed colonising Australia, but instead of conventional settlers, he would send out convicts as pioneers. This plan, he contended, would solve the crisis in Britain's overflowing jails.

For most of the 18th century, the British had disposed of troublesome convicts by banishing them to North America. With the American Revolution, though, this destination was no longer an option. The motherland's prisons could not cope, and the river hulks that were used as floating jails threatened to overflow with riots and disease.

In May 1787 the British government began the transportation of criminals to Australia. The programme was to endure for 80 years. In that time more than 160,000 convicts were shipped to a new life Down Under.

THE FIRST FLEET

A retired naval officer, Captain Arthur Phillip, was put in command of the first fleet of 11 sailing vessels carrying nearly 1,500 people – more than half of them convicts – on an eight-month voyage from Portsmouth to New South Wales. Against the odds, the convoy was a success.

Captain Phillip (now with the title Governor)

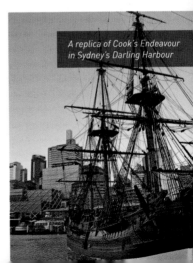

A replica of Cook's Endeavour in Sydney's Darling Harbour

came ashore in full ceremonial dress but unarmed. Spear-toting Aborigines milled about like an unwelcoming committee. A lieutenant on the flagship wrote: 'I think it is very easy to conceive the ridiculous figure we must appear to these poor creatures, who were perfectly naked.'

As the truth about Botany Bay was unveiled, Cook's rosy claims faded to bleak. The expedition's officers were appalled to discover that there was no shelter from east winds, that much of the alleged meadowland was actually swamp and that there was not enough fresh water to go around.

Luckily, the next best thing to paradise was waiting just around the corner. Governor Phillip and a reconnaissance party sailed 20km (12 miles) up the coast and discovered what Fleet Surgeon John White called 'the finest and most extensive harbour in the universe', big enough to provide 'safe anchorage for all the navies of Europe'. It was also strikingly beautiful. Today it is decorated with an opera house and a bridge and is called Sydney Harbour. The fleet reassembled at Sydney Cove on 26 January 1788 (the date is marked every year as the Australian national holiday), and the British flag was raised over the colony.

London's great expectations took for granted that New South Wales would be instantly self-sufficient. Real life fell dangerously short of the theory. The Sydney summer was too hot for exertion, and even if the

Captain James Cook, as portrayed by Nathaniel Dance

convicts had genuinely wanted to pitch in, the soil was unpromising. In any event, most of the outcasts were city-bred and didn't know the difference between a hoe and a sickle. Livestock died or disappeared in the bush.

Shipwrecks and delays in London meant that relief supplies were delayed for nearly two years, causing increasing desperation. As food dwindled, rations were cut. Prisoners caught stealing food were flogged. Finally, to set an example, the Governor ordered a food looter to be hanged.

In June 1790, to all-round jubilation, the supply ship *Lady Juliana* reached Sydney harbour and the long fast ended. As agriculture finally began to blossom, many thousands of new prisoners were shipped out. And even voluntary settlers chose Australia as the land of their future.

ENTER CAPTAIN BLIGH

When Governor Phillip retired, the colony's top army officer, Major Francis Grose, took over. His army subordinates fared very well under the new regime, which encouraged free enterprise. The officers soon found profitable sidelines, usually at the expense of the British taxpayers. The army's monopoly on the sale of rum made quick fortunes; under some tipsy economic law, rum began to replace money as Australia's medium of exchange. Even prisoners were paid in alcohol for their extracurricular jobs.

As news of widespread hanky-panky reached London, the government responded by sending out a well-known disciplinarian to shake up the rum-sodden militia. He was Captain William Bligh, victim of the notorious mutiny on HMS *Bounty* seven years earlier. Bligh meant to put fear into the hearts of backsliding officers, but his explosive temper was beyond control. His New South Wales victims nicknamed the new governor Caligula and plotted treason.

Bligh was deposed by a group of insurgent officers on 26 January 1808, as the colony toasted its 20th anniversary. The

Rum Rebellion, as the mutiny was dubbed, led to a radical reorganisation and reshuffle in personnel. But the inevitable court-martial seemed to take into account how Bligh's personality and methods had galled his subordinates. The mutineers were finally punished by more than a rap on the knuckles, but less than they might have expected.

OPENING A CONTINENT

New South Wales, under Governor Lachlan Macquarie (served 1809–21), overcame the stigma of a penal colony and became a land of opportunity. The idealistic army officer organised the building of schools, a hospital and a courthouse, and roads to link them. As a method of inspiration for exiles to 'go straight' and win emancipation, Macquarie appointed an ex-convict as Justice of the Peace. Then he invited some of the others to dinner, much to the horror of the local elite. One of the criminals

⊘ BRAVE BUT FALLIBLE

Captain William Bligh never won any popularity contests, but historians believe that he was not as bad as is sometimes thought. Before his career in Australia, he had a distinguished record: he had circumnavigated the globe with James Cook, fought under Horatio Nelson at the Battle of Copenhagen, and shown evidence of a superhuman survival instinct when the *Bounty* mutineers abandoned him in the Pacific. Thanks to his courage, his skill as a navigator, and good fortune, he survived a voyage of 5,823km (3,618 miles) in a lifeboat. By coincidence he had also been involved in another serious naval mutiny, in 1797, before being appointed Governor of New South Wales to re-establish discipline. This captain, immortalised by Hollywood, eventually reached the rank of Rear Admiral.

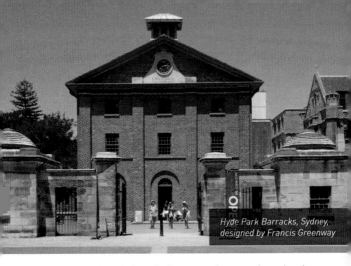

Hyde Park Barracks, Sydney, designed by Francis Greenway

Macquarie pardoned, Francis Greenway, became the colony's prolific official architect.

Some of the ex-convicts fared so well under Macquarie's progressive policies that he was accused of pampering the criminal class. The authorities in London ordered tougher punishment, and the total separation of prisoners from the rest of the population. All this led to long-lasting conflict between reformed criminals and their children on one side and a privileged class of immigrants on the other. Nowadays, the shoe is firmly on the other foot: descendants of First Fleet convicts often express the same kind of pride as Americans of *Mayflower* ancestry.

The biggest problem for Governor Macquarie and his immediate successors was the colony's position on the edge of the sea. There was not enough land to provide food for the expanding population. The Blue Mountains, which boxed in Sydney Cove, seemed a hopeless barrier. Every attempt to break through the labyrinth of steep valleys failed. Then, in 1813, explorers Blaxland, Wentworth and Lawson had the unconventional idea of crossing the peaks rather than the valleys. It worked. Beyond the Blue Mountains they discovered a land of plenty – endless plains that would support a great new society.

Other adventurers opened new territories. Land was either confiscated or bought from indigenous tribesmen: for 400 sq km (150 sq miles) of what is now Melbourne, the entrepreneurs gave the Aborigines a wagonload of clothing and blankets, together with 30 knives, 12 tomahawks, 10 mirrors, 12 pairs of scissors and 23kg (50lb) of flour. By the middle of the 19th century, thousands of settlers had poured into Australia and all of the present state capitals were on the map.

AGE OF GOLD

In his understandable enthusiasm, prospector Edward Hargraves slightly overstated the case when he declared: 'This is a memorable day in the history of New South Wales. I shall be a baronet.' The

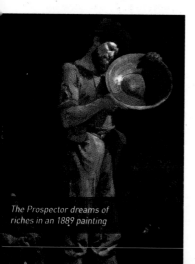

The Prospector dreams of riches in an 1889 painting

year was 1851. The place was near Bathurst, approximately 210km (130 miles) west of Sydney. Hargraves' audience consisted of one speechless colleague. The occasion was the discovery of gold in Australia.

At almost the same time, prospectors from Melbourne struck gold in Ballarat. With two colonies – New South Wales and Victoria – sharing in the boom, adventurers streamed in from Europe and America. By the year 1860, Australia's population had reached a total of one million. Thirty-three years later the bonanza became a coast-to-coast celebration when gold was discovered in Kalgoorlie in Western Australia.

Life in the gold fields was rugged, conditions aggravated by climate, flies and tax collectors. Whether big winners or small losers, all the diggers had to pay the same licence fee. Enforcement and fines were needlessly strict. Justice, the miners felt, was tilted against them. So they burned their licences and demonstrated for voting rights and other reforms. In the subsequent siege of the Eureka Stockade in Ballarat in 1854, troops were ordered to attack the demonstrators. There was heavy loss of life, and the licence fee was abandoned.

Another riot, in 1861, pitted the white prospectors against Chinese miners, who were resented for their foreignness, strong work ethic and frugality. At Lambing Flat, New South Wales, thousands of whites whipped and clubbed a community of Chinese. Police, troops and finally the courts were lenient on the attackers. It was the worst of several race riots.

ROGUES ON THE RANGE

Transportation of convicts finally ended in 1868, when London had to admit that the threat of exile in Australia was no deterrent to crime. In Australia itself, crime was always a problem; nobody really expected every last sinner to go straight as soon as he arrived. Several wily characters, often escaped convicts, became bushrangers, the local version of highwaymen. They occasionally attracted sympathy from Outback folk because they tended to rob the rich and flout authority. As the crimes grew more ambitious or outrageous, their fame was frozen into legend.

The saga of Ned Kelly (1854–80) reads like Robin Hood gone sour. The Kelly gang preyed on bankers rather than humble farmers, and Kelly's imaginative operations could be spectacular, but he killed three policemen and still divides a nation's opinion

– some regard him as a hero, others a murderer. Wounded in a shootout while wearing a suit of homemade armour, Kelly was captured alive. Sentenced to death, he cheekily invited the judge to meet him in the hereafter. Two weeks after Kelly was hanged, the judge died.

AN INDEPENDENT NATION

Having received the blessing of Queen Victoria, the colonies of Australia formed a new nation, the Commonwealth of Australia, on New Year's Day 1901. This federation retained the Queen as head of state, and bowed to the parliament and Privy Council in London.

Loyalty to the British Empire was tested twice, extravagantly, in the world wars. The Gallipoli campaign in 1915–16 was the first and most memorable single disaster for Australian troops. By the end of World War I, over 200,000 Australians – two-thirds of the expeditionary force – had been killed or wounded.

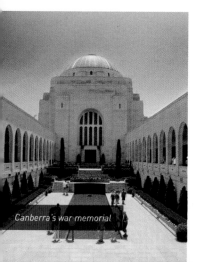
Canberra's war memorial

Combat came closer to home in World War II, when Japanese planes repeatedly bombed Darwin, enemy submarines penetrated Sydney harbour and sank a ferry (the torpedo had been fired at the American warship USS *Chicago*), ships were sunk off the Australian coast and a couple of shells hit Sydney's eastern suburbs. American forces under General MacArthur arrived in Australia in 1942 and a US force supported by Australia defeated the

Japanese decisively in the Battle of the Coral Sea in May of that year. The statistics: 27,000 Australian servicemen died in action on the European and Asian fronts, and nearly 8,000 more died as prisoners of Japan.

> ### Greek city?
>
> Thanks to its immigrant population, Melbourne is often called the third greatest Greek city, after Athens and Thessaloniki.

After the war, Britain aligned itself with Europe and downgraded its ties with the old Empire. As Britain's regional power declined, Australia boosted its alliance with the US. Australian troops (more than 40,000 of them) fought alongside Americans in Vietnam, sparking vehement anti-war protests in Sydney and other Australian cities. Australian Prime Minister Harold Holt introduced the draft and promised US President Lyndon B. Johnson that Australia would go 'all the way with LBJ'. Holt disappeared in 1967 while swimming at Cheviot Beach south of Melbourne; it is believed he was caught in the undertow and swept out to sea.

The tilt towards the US and Asia also showed up in Australia's balance of trade. Prior to World War II, 42 percent of Australia's overseas trade was with Britain. Today, Australia's top 10 export markets include Japan, Singapore, China, Korea, Taiwan, India and Thailand. Japan buys almost one fifth of Australia's total merchandise exports. Among non-Asian markets, the most significant for Australian exporters are the US, New Zealand and Britain.

CULTURAL CHANGES

Another obvious change in orientation is the racial and national background of Australians. Before World War II, 98 percent of the population was of British or Irish birth or descent. As for immigrants, 81 percent of Australia's overseas-born population came from the main English-speaking countries (Britain, Ireland, New Zealand, South

Africa, Canada and the US). Since then, the fortress walls of the infamous 'White Australia' immigration policy (enacted in 1901 to maintain racial purity) have been torn down under the slogan 'Populate or Perish.' Australia has seen immigration from many countries including Italy, Greece, Malta, the former Yugoslavia, Vietnam, Germany, the Netherlands, the Philippines, Malaysia, Lebanon, Turkey, Hong Kong, China, South Africa, Sudan, Afghanistan and Iraq.

Since 1945, Australia has accepted 7 million people as new settlers – about 660,000 of whom arrived under humanitarian programmes – creating a culturally diverse nation. Nearly a quarter of Australia's population is overseas-born. By 2006, only 34 percent of the overseas-born population had been born in English-speaking countries.

Australia has had a less than comfortable relationship with its own indigenous peoples, the Aborigines and Torres Strait Islanders. Together, they make up just three percent of the population (about 90 percent of which are Aborigines). Aborigines were not permitted

Australia's fallen soldiers are remembered on Anzac Day

to vote in national elections until 1962, and were not included in the census until 1967. Worse, from the late 19th century until about 1970, governments forcibly removed as many as 100,000 Aboriginal children, mainly of mixed race, from their families. The children – later dubbed the Stolen Generations – were taken to church missions, orphanages and foster homes.

In 1990, a government-appointed commission gave Australia's indigenous peoples the power to make decisions on social and other matters that affect them. In 1993, there were further moves towards reconciliation, with legislation effectively nullifying the doctrine of *terra nullius* ('uninhabited land'), which had deemed Australia to be empty at the time of European settlement and, by default, the property of the Crown. The court ruling recognised that Aborigines may hold common law rights or 'native title' to land.

Support continues to grow for a treaty with the Aboriginal people to foster national unity. In 2000, in cities throughout Australia, many thousands of citizens marched to demand that the government formally apologise to the Stolen Generations, to begin a process of reconciliation. In Sydney, 250,000 people marched for the cause. However, no progress on the issue was made until February 2008, when Labor prime minister Kevin Rudd issued an apology.

Australia entered the 21st century in an upbeat mood. In the late 2000s, its economy weathered the global financial crisis better than most other Western economies, avoiding recession thanks to targeted stimulus spending by the government and a resilient mining boom driven by rising demand for coal and iron ore in China.

Politically, however, all was not well. When Kevin Rudd proposed a carbon pollution reduction scheme and a mineral resources tax on mining companies' profits, his public popularity dipped and soon after so did his support from parliamentary colleagues. In June 2010, his deputy Julia Gillard replaced him, becoming Australia's first female prime minister. Following the August 2010 federal election, Julia Gillard formed a minority Labor government with

The Union flag still occupies a quarter of the Australian flag

the support of three independent members and the sole member representing the Australian Greens in the House of Representatives.

After three years of constant media speculation about a potential comeback, the political pantomime went full circle and Rudd was reinstated as Labor leader and Australian Prime Minister in June 2013, but the Liberal Party led by Tony Abbott won a decisive victory in the general election in September that year. Abbott rode in on the back of promises that he would roll back the carbon tax and 'stop the boats' (meaning refugees). In 2014 his government signed off on a proposal to increase the number of boats (in the shape of large tankers) that can sail across the waters of the Great Barrier Reef, with the expansion of deepwater coal mining activity in the World Heritage area (including some dredging), and indicated that Tasmania's National Parks (some of which are also World Heritage listed) are 'open for business' for the forestry industry – two policies that were likely to set the battlelines for the next fight between big business and environmentalists.

In September 2015, Abbott was defeated in a leadership ballot and replaced as the Prime Minister by Malcolm Turnbull. Soon after, there was a double dissolution federal election held in 2016. Malcolm Turnbull once again became the Prime Minister of Australia. It was the first double dissolution election since the 1987 election and the first under a new voting system for the Senate that replaced group voting tickets with optional preferential voting.

HISTORICAL LANDMARKS

50,000 BC The Aborigines arrive on the Australian continent.

1606 Willem Jansz is the first European to land.

1642 Abel Tasman discovers Tasmania and New Zealand.

1770 Lieutenant James Cook explores the east coast of Australia.

1788 Britain establishes a penal colony in Sydney Cove.

1808 The 'Rum Rebellion' overthrows Captain William Bligh.

1851 Gold is discovered in New South Wales.

1854 Battle of the Eureka Stockade, Ballarat.

1901 Six colonies federated into the Commonwealth of Australia.

1914–18 330,000 Australians serve in WWI; 60,000 are killed, 156,000 wounded.

1917 Opening of the transcontinental railway.

1927 Federal parliament moves from Melbourne to Canberra.

1939–45 WWII: Australian Air Force active in Britain; navy operates in Mediterranean; soldiers fight in North Africa and the Pacific.

1956 Olympic Games held in Melbourne. First Australian TV.

1960 Australia grants citizenship to Aborigines.

1962 Aborigines allowed to vote in federal elections.

1973 Sydney Opera House is finally completed.

1985 Uluru and Kata Tjuta are returned to Aboriginal owners.

1993 The Aborigines' right to own land is recognised.

2000 Olympic Games in Sydney.

2008 Prime Minister Rudd apologises to the Stolen Generations.

2009 173 people killed by devastating bush fires in Victoria.

2010 Julia Gillard becomes Australia's first female prime minister.

2011 Brisbane and nearby areas experience major flooding in January, and Severe Tropical Cyclone Yasi tears through North Queensland in February.

2013 Australian Liberal Party returned to Government.

2015 The Liberal/National Coalition wins the federal election.

2016 Agreement made for refugees held in detention centres on Pacific islands to be resettled in the US in a 'one-off deal'. The first double dissolution election since 1987 is won by the Liberal/National Coalition.

2017 Cyclone Debbie causes major flooding across Queensland and northern New South Wales.

Kangaroo on the beach at Lucky Bay, WA

WHERE TO GO

Deciding where to go and what to see in Australia may be the hardest part of the journey. How can you squeeze so much into a limited time? Where do you go in such a vast country? And what do you stop off to see?

About 54 million passengers a year fly Australia's domestic airline routes. Budget airlines make flying from city to city an affordable option, although it's best to plan ahead to get the best fares and flight times. Alternatives are slower, but often more revealing. Try the transcontinental trains and the long-distance buses, some of which are equipped for luxury travel.

Since you probably can't see all of it, you'll have to arrange your tour of Australia to concentrate on seeing a manageable slice or two of the continent. Planning any itinerary requires compromise, depending on the time and funds you have available, the season, your special interests and your choice of gateway city. Sydney is the main gateway into Australia, but some airlines allow you to arrive in Cairns, for example, and depart from Sydney or Perth.

This section of the guide is arranged according to the geography of Australia's states. Although there is no visible difference between the red deserts of the Northern Territory and those of South Australia, it's practical to consider them in the context of the political frontiers. Besides, the way that history and chance carved Australia into states comes close to providing a fairly natural division into sightseeing regions.

In each state or territory we start with the capital city gateway and fan out from there. We begin where European settlement of Australia began, at Sydney Cove. After a side trip to the federal capital, Canberra, we continue beyond New South Wales, in an anti-clockwise circuit from Queensland to Victoria, ending with a look at the continent's lovely green footnote, Tasmania.

NEW SOUTH WALES

Sydney can't help but dominate New South Wales (NSW), if only because most of the state's population lives in the capital. However, beyond the metropolis, the state – six times the size of England – is a varied patchwork of terrain, lurching from dairyland and desert to vineyards and craggy mountains.

SYDNEY

Sydney ❶ is Australia's oldest, liveliest and biggest city (total population around 5 million). If the world had a lifestyle capital, Sydney would be a strong contender –ironic considering it began life as a British penal colony. Sydney is sun-drenched, brawny, energetic, fun loving and outdoor obsessed. The city ranks well on international lists of favourite tourist destinations; its residents know this and they revel in it. After hours – and Sydneysiders do live for the after hours – Sydney offers every imaginable cosmopolitan delight. It's a sunny coincidence that beaches famous for surfing and scenery are only minutes away.

Sydney Harbour has been stealing the show ever since the first convicts arrived in 1788. For a quick appreciation of the intricacies of **Port Jackson** (the official name for Sydney Harbour), gaze out from the top of Sydney Tower, Sydney's tallest building. From here you can see the clear blue

View from Sydney's Market Street

Sydney, with the famous Opera House in the foreground

tentacles of water stretching from the South Pacific into the heart of the city. Schools of sailing boats patrol the harbour, shattering the reflection of skyscrapers, the classic Sydney Harbour Bridge and the iconic opera house. It's a pity that James Cook never noticed this glorious setting as he sailed right past on his way home to England from Botany Bay. Sydney Harbour National Park fringes a long, leafy stretch of the northern side of the harbour and also includes some harbour islands and a chunk of the southern foreshore. For information about harbour sights, see page 59. Exploring Sydney Harbour is as easy as jumping on a commuter ferry or taking a sightseeing tour. Most tours – by land or sea – leave from Circular Quay.

Most of the world's great cities have a famous landmark that serves as an instantly recognisable symbol. Sydney has two: the perfect steel arch of Sydney Harbour Bridge and the billowing shell-like roofs of the Sydney Opera House. That's what happens when engineers and architects embellish a harbour coveted by artists as well as admirals.

Sydney Opera House

There's a real sense of occasion and style about the structure of the **Sydney Opera House** Ⓐ (www.sydneyoperahouse.com; guided one-hour tours daily, every half-hour 9am–5pm), both inside and out. This unique building, covered in a million tiles, has achieved the seemingly impossible by improving a virtually perfect harbour. Yet its controversial architect left the country in a huff at an early stage of the building's construction.

Pre-opera house, the promontory was the location of a tram depot, but in the 1950s the government of New South Wales decided to build a performing arts centre on the site. In 1957, a Danish architect called Jørn Utzon won an international competition to design the building. His novel plan included problems of spherical geometry so tricky that he actually chopped up a wooden sphere to prove it could be done. The shell of the complex was almost complete when Utzon walked out in 1966 due to pressure from the state government; the interior, which was in dispute, became the work of a committee. Despite this, from the tip of its highest roof (67 metres/220ft above sea level) to the Drama Theatre's orchestra pit (more than a fathom below sea level), this place oozes grace, taste and class.

In 2002, Utzon was awarded the Pritzker Prize, architecture's version of the Nobel Prize, and in 2004 a room in the Opera House was named after him, complete with a 14-metre long, floor-to-ceiling woollen tapestry designed by the architect installed inside. But Utzon never returned to Sydney; he died in 2008 without ever laying eyes on his finished masterpiece.

Circular Quay

Although cruise ships and water taxis also dock here at **Circular Quay** Ⓑ (short for Semi-Circular Quay, as it was more accurately originally named), most of the action involves ferries, which sail to various destinations including the zoo (see page 59) and seaside suburbs such as Manly (see page 61). The quay's high-paced

flow of human traffic includes hasty travellers, leisurely sightseers, street musicians, artists, hawkers and people just 'hanging
out'. Whether you see Australia's busiest harbour from the deck
of a luxury liner, a sightseeing boat, or a humble ferry, don't miss
experiencing this invigorating angle on the city's skyline.

The Rocks

To see where it all began, stroll through the charming streets of **The
Rocks** ⓒ (www.therocks.com), just west of Circular Quay. You can
take a 90-minute guided walking tour (tel: 02-9247 6678 to book) or
conduct your own tour. Here modern Australia's founding fathers –
mostly convicts who had been charged with anything from shoplifting
to major forgery – came ashore in 1788 to build the colony of New
South Wales. This historic waterfront district has everything a traveller could want: lovely views at long and short range, moody old buildings, cheerful plazas and plenty of distractions in the way of shopping,

Sailing through the Harbour

Susannah Place is an example of a working-class terrace

eating and drinking. There are plenty of tourists too.

But it nearly was not so. The Rocks was once one of Sydney's most squalid and dangerous quarters, a Dickensian warren of warehouses, grog shops and brothels, where the rum was laced with tobacco juice and the larrikin 'razor gangs' preyed on the unwary. An outbreak of bubonic plague in 1900 was another low-light in The Rocks' sordid history.

The whole area was due to be levelled for redevelopment in the 1970s, but there was fierce resistance from residents and academics, and the project was thwarted when the construction unions, led by activist Jack Mundey, refused to start work. This was the beginning of the Green movement to preserve the antiquities and atmospheric elements of Old Sydney.

A wide range of local leaflets and maps is on offer at the **Sydney Visitor Centre** (corner Argyle and Playfair streets; www.therocks. com; daily 9.30am–5.30pm). You can book tours there as well.

Nearby, **Cadman's Cottage** is central Sydney's oldest (1816) surviving house – a simple stone cottage occupied for many years by the government's official boatsman. It's now the information centre for Sydney Harbour National Park. Not far away, the **Museum of Contemporary Art** (www.mca.com.au; daily 10am–5pm; free) gives new life to an Art Deco building. The museum's collection ranges from Aboriginal bark paintings to the latest – and strangest – installation works. There are also plenty of touring exhibitions. The café on the terrace (with harbour view) is excellent.

Just south of The Rocks, on Bridge Street on the site of the first Government House, the fascinating **Museum of Sydney** (daily 10am–5pm; charge) promises to take visitors on 'a journey of discovery' from 1788 to the present day.

North of Cadman's Cottage are solid 19th-century bond stores, now converted to offices and shops such as **Campbell's Storehouse** (which sells food, souvenirs, arts and crafts). Heading west from Cadman's Cottage you'll arrive at the similar **Argyle Stores**. Beyond is the **Argyle Cut**, a massive gap through the sandstone cliffs that was initially hacked out by convict labour-gangs using pickaxes.

At the top of Argyle Cut, Cumberland Street provides pedestrian access to Sydney Harbour Bridge via a set of steps. An unusual vantage point for viewing the bridge, the harbour and the skyline – from the top of one of the bridge's massive pylons – can be accessed here. The **Pylon Lookout** (www.pylonlookout.com.au; daily 10am–5pm; charge) is in the southeast tower, which also contains a museum.

Not far away, the **Australian Hotel**, a friendly pub in the older Aussie tradition, stocks beers from every state in the country. It is one of only two pubs in Sydney to serve Bavarian-style unfiltered beers created by brewer Geoff Scharer, acclaimed as the best in Australia.

A little further on, in Argyle Place, you will find a neat row of terraced houses straight out of Georgian England. Two other old pubs in this area deserve mention. The first, the quaint **Hero of**

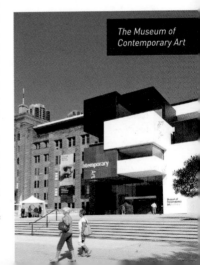

The Museum of Contemporary Art

Waterloo at 81 Lower Fort Street, was built in 1843 on top of a maze of subterranean cellars through which drunken patrons were conveyed to be sold as crew to unscrupulous sea captains; that practice has died out but the cellars remain. The second, the **Lord Nelson Brewery Hotel**, a square sandstone block of a building at the corner of Kent and Argyle Street, was built around 1840 and has maintained something of a British naval atmosphere ever since. It brews its own beers, some of them pretty potent.

For history without the refreshments, visit the sandstone Garrison Church, officially named the **Holy Trinity Anglican Church**, which dates from the early 1840s. As the unofficial name indicates, it was the church for members of the garrison regiment, the men in charge of the convict colony. It's now a fashionable place to get married.

At the start of George Street, close to the Irish-influenced Mercantile Hotel, **The Rocks Market** (Sat–Sun 10am–5pm) takes place every weekend under a 150-metre (492-ft) long canopy. Street

Pulling pints at the Lord Nelson Hotel

entertainers perform, while stall-holders sell crafts, souvenirs, toys and gifts. Nearby, Customs Officers Stairs lead down to some charming harbour-side restaurants housed in old bond stores, fronting **Campbells Cove**. Just across the harbour is the Opera House.

Overhanging The Rocks, **Observatory Park** is a perfect place from which to gaze at the sky or at Sydney Harbour. **Observatory Hill** here is the highest point in the city, visible for kilometres around. Since the middle of the 19th century, every day at 1pm precisely, a ball is dropped from the top of a mast to enable sea captains to check their chronometers. **Sydney Observatory** (www. sydneyobservatory.com.au; daily 10am–5pm) is now a museum of astronomy, and opens every evening (times vary according to season) for talks, films and star-gazing (bookings, tel: 02-9217 0111).

Another favourite lookout is **Dawes Point Park**, where a scattering of old cannons provides the perfect perch for watching the ferries and sailing boats.

Here, you're in the shadow of the **Sydney Harbour Bridge D**, with its drive-through stone pylons (purely ornamental) and colossal steel arch. The bridge stars on television each New Year's Eve, when it serves as a platform for a spectacular fireworks display to bid farewell to the old year and welcome in the new. Pyrotechnics are fired from the arch and more fireworks on the road-span create a Niagara-like cascade into Sydney Harbour.

Linking the city and the north, the bridge's single arch is 503 metres (1,650ft) across – wide enough to carry eight lanes of cars and two railway tracks, as well as lanes for pedestrians and cyclists. When it was built, during the Great Depression, Sydneysiders called the bridge the Iron Lung, because it kept a lot of people 'breathing' – by giving them jobs. It takes 10 years to repaint the steel-grey bridge, at the end of which it's time to start again. To ease traffic congestion a tunnel has also been built under the harbour.

A company called BridgeClimb (tel: 02-8274 7777; www.bridge climb.com.au; charge) conducts guided walks for small groups over

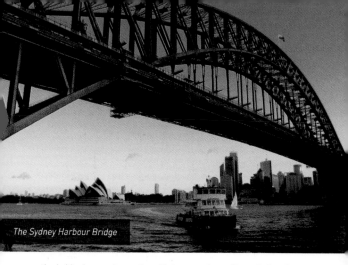

The Sydney Harbour Bridge

the bridge's massive arches. Not across the walkway below, but over the arches above. For decades, groups of daredevils had been doing this illicitly. Since the legal climb began in 1998 the waiting list has grown quite long and it pays to book your climb as far in advance as you can. You can even do the climb at dawn, twilight or at night, though excursions are understandably postponed during electrical storms. It's not a cheap thrill: tickets start from A$248, and cost more for twilight or dawn climbs or at weekends (minimum age 10).

City Centre

A similar tour operates from the top of **Sydney Tower** Ⓔ (Centre-point, corner of Pitt and Market streets; tel: 1800-258 693; www.sydneytowereye.com.au; daily 9am–10pm, ; charge). Skywalk offers walks outside the tower's turret, the city's highest vantage point, at 305 metres (1,001ft) above the street. Those without a head for heights can still take in the view; in the lifts it takes only 40 seconds to reach the observation decks, where amateur photographers get that glazed look as they peer through the tinted windows to unlimited horizons. On a flawless day you can see all the way north to Terrigal and south to Wollongong, far out to sea to the east, and as far west as the Blue Mountains. Otherwise, look down at the seething shopping streets around the tower. Pedestrians-only **Pitt Street Mall** is one of the city's main retail centres, home to department stores and shops of all kinds. The **Strand Arcade**, which runs off the Mall, is a grand old shopping arcade full of upmarket boutiques.

A short distance towards the harbour is the city's main square, **Martin Place**, flanked by the imposing Victorian **General Post Office** (GPO) building. This has been imaginatively converted into a stylish modern complex including a five-star hotel.

From the same era, but even grander, the sandstone **Queen Victoria Building** ❻ (www.qvb.com.au; Mon–Sat 9am–6pm, Thur 9am–9pm, Sun 11am–5pm) occupies a whole block on George Street opposite the Town Hall. The Byzantine-style 'QVB' began as a municipal market and commercial centre, including a hotel and a concert hall, topped by statues and some 21 domes.

Built in 1898 to commemorate Queen Victoria's Golden Jubilee, it was faithfully restored in the 1980s to create a magnificent all-weather shopping centre housing nearly 200 chic boutiques, cafés and restaurants, in a cool and unhurried atmosphere of period charm. Pierre Cardin called it 'the most beautiful shopping centre in the world'. The **Galeries** (www.thegaleries. com), across George Street, offer yet more shopping opportunities in a modern space.

Next door to the QVB, Sydney's **Town Hall** (www.syd neytownhall.com.au; daily 9am–5pm) enlivens a site that used to be a cemetery. The

Pipped at the post

In 1932, at the opening ceremony of the Harbour Bridge, an Irish-born member of a proto-fascist group, Francis Edward de Groot, rode up on a horse and sliced through the ribbon with a sword before the left-wing premier of NSW, Jack Lang, could cut it.

The ornate Queen Victoria Building

Victorian-era building, home of the city council, is also used for concerts and exhibitions. The Anglican **St Andrew's Cathedral** next to it dates from 1868.

Chinatown and Darling Harbour

After dark, young Sydneysiders flock to the section of George Street heading south from the Town Hall, lined with video entertainment arcades, fast-food joints and a cinema complex. Sydney's fledgling Spanish Quarter begins nearby on the corner of George Street and Liverpool Street – there's a choice of tapas bars here.

In the adjacent Chinatown district, gourmets can enjoy the delights of Peking, Cantonese and Szechuan cuisine. The substantial local Chinese community is joined here by Sydneysiders and tourists enjoying the Chinese cafés, restaurants and shops selling exotic spices and knick-knacks. The district's centrepiece is **Dixon Street**, a pedestrian zone framed by ceremonial gates.

If you're in the area at the right time, check out **Paddy's Market** in Hay Street (Wed–Sun 10am–6pm), a brick building beneath a skyscraper called Market City. Paddy's is full of stalls selling almost anything from seashells and sunglasses to fruit and vegetables. Market City has plenty of Chinese and other Asian eateries to satisfy hunger pangs.

Nearby, the modern leisure precinct of **Darling Harbour** is well stocked with shops, restaurants and attractions, and a light rail system links it to more central areas. On the city side of Darling Harbour lie **Cockle Bay Wharf** and **King Street Wharf**, complexes of bars and restaurants. These areas have proved much more popular than the shopping and dining complex overlooking the harbour on the western side, mainly because they are easier to reach on foot from downtown Sydney.

Not far away, **Sea Life Sydney Aquarium** G (www.sydney aquarium.com.au; daily 9.30am–6pm; charge), relaunched as a Sea Life Centre in 2012 after a A$10 million refurbishment, is one of the largest aquariums in the world. In its oceanarium, large sharks weigh up to 300kg (660lb) and measure over 3.5 metres (11ft) long. The Great Barrier Reef Complex is home to hundreds of colourful species, and a visit there is the closest thing to diving on the actual reef. The adjacent **Sydney Wildlife World** (www.sydneywildlifeworld.com.au; daily 9.30am–5pm; charge) is a mini-zoo showcasing a selection of native fauna, from lizards and snakes to parrots and wallabies. The star attractions, however, are the koalas, which, for an

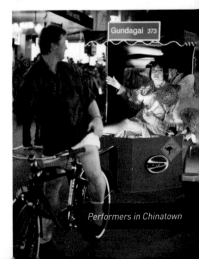

Performers in Chinatown

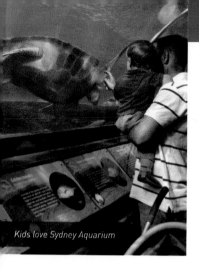
Kids love Sydney Aquarium

extra fee, you can have your photo taken with.

Other nearby attractions include the Australian **National Maritime Museum** (www.anmm.gov.au; daily 9.30am–5pm, till 6pm in Jan; charge), a Chinese garden (daily 9.30am–5pm), and an IMAX cinema. A new **International Convention Centre** was opened in 2016 at Darling Harbour. Beyond the Maritime Museum, in Pyrmont, is **Star City Casino** (daily 24 hours).

Parks and gardens

Although Sydney's lush **Hyde Park** is only a fraction the size of its namesake in London, it still provides the same sort of green relief. Like most big-city parks, however, it should be avoided after sunset. The most formal feature of the semi-formal gardens, the **Anzac War Memorial**, commemorates the World War I fighters in monumental Art Deco style, with later acknowledgments to World War II soldiers.

Sightseers interested in old churches should mark a few targets on the edge of Hyde Park. To the north, the early colonial **St James' Church** in Queens Square was the work of the convict architect Francis Greenway. Just across College Street on the east is the Catholic **St Mary's Cathedral**.

You can view the cathedral's spires while immersed in a swimming pool next door at **Cook + Phillip Park** Aquatic and Fitness Centre (www.cookandphillip.org.au; Mon–Fri 6am–10pm, Sat–Sun and public holidays 7am–8pm; charge). You can't readily see the complex from the street, yet when you're inside, its huge windows offer amazing views and let in lots of light. There are three pools – one with a wave machine. There's a café inside, or, if you want to eat alfresco, Bodhi's vegan restaurant does good business just outside.

The ornate **Great Synagogue** (tours Tue and Thur at noon) faces the park across Elizabeth Street. Jews have lived in Sydney since the arrival of the first shipment of prisoners.

The **Australian Museum**  (tel: 02-9320 6000; http://australian museum.net.au; daily 9.30am–5pm; charge) on 1 William Street specialises in natural history and anthropology, and has lots of activities and events suitable for inquisitive minds. Highlights include a dinosaur gallery (complete with life-size models and 10 complete skeletons), an exhibit of Australia's megafauna (giant-sized marsupials and flightless birds), a hands-on plant and animal identification centre, a gallery devoted to Australia's unique ecosystems, the Indigenous Australians exhibition, and a human evolution gallery.

Hyde Park

Hyde Park Barracks (http://sydneylivingmuseums.com.au; daily 10am–5pm; charge), designed by Greenway and located between Hyde Park and the Botanic Gardens, is now a museum of social history. On the top floor, one large room features a reconstruction of the dormitory life of the prisoners who once slept there. Next door, the **Mint** (10 Macquarie St; tel: 02-8239 2288; http://sydney livingmuseums.com.au; daily 9.30am–5pm; free) processed gold-rush bullion in the mid-19th century.

Another large park adjacent to Hyde Park is called the **Domain**, where concerts are held in summer. On one side of the Domain is the **Art Gallery of New South Wales** ❶ (www.artgallery.nsw.gov. au; daily 10am–5pm; free, charge for exhibitions) consisting of a formal exterior decorated with much bronze statuary and a modern extension that infuses light into the building and provides sweeping views of east Sydney, part of the harbour, and the suburb of Woolloomooloo. An afternoon at the art gallery will give you a crash

Art Gallery of New South Wales

course in more than a century of traditional and modern Australian art. The **Yiribana Gallery** is devoted to Aboriginal art and Torres Islander art (guided tours daily 1pm; free).

The **Royal Botanic Gardens** ❶ (www.rbgsyd.nsw.gov.au; daily 7am–sunset; free guided walks daily at 10.30am) began as a different sort of garden; here the early colonists tried – with very limited success – to grow vegetables. Only a few steps from the busy skyscraper-world of downtown Sydney, you can relax in the shade of Moreton Bay fig trees, palms or mahoganies, or enter the Sydney Tropical Centre (daily 10am–4pm; charge; temporarily closed for redevelopment), two glass pyramids full of orchids and other tropical beauties. Near the Tropical Centre, overlooking the duck pond, is a café-restaurant where you can relax in peaceful surroundings.

There are several entrances to the gardens and many paths; the most popular entrance is by the Opera House. From here the gardens curve down around Farm Cove to a peninsula called **Mrs Macquarie's Chair**. The lady thus immortalised, the wife of the go-ahead second governor, used to admire the view from here. Nearby is the venue for the summer season of outdoor films that are shown here during the Sydney Festival (www.sydneyfestival.org.au) and during the St George OpenAir Cinema season (January to the end of February; www.stgeorgeopenair.com.au). There's a lot to see in the Gardens, and if you're feeling tired, you can take advantage of the hop-on hop-off Trackless Train, which does a 20-minute loop between the Opera House Gate and the Woolloomooloo Gate near the Art Gallery.

Centennial Park, most easily reached from the eastern end of Oxford Street in the inner-city suburb of **Paddington**, has provided greenery and fresh air to city folk since 1888, when it was dedicated – on the centenary of Australia's foundation – to 'the enjoyment of the people of New South Wales forever'. The park's 220 hectares (544 acres) of trees, lawns, duck ponds, rose gardens and bridle-paths are visited by about 3 million people a year, who cycle, roller-blade, walk dogs, feed birds, play sports, fly kites, picnic and barbecue.

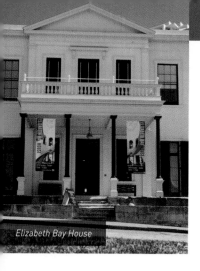
Elizabeth Bay House

If you fancy a ride on the bridle path, horse rental can be arranged from Moore Park Stables (tel: 02-9360 8747; www.mooreparkstables.com.au). Bicycles and pedal-carts can be hired from Centennial Park Cycles (tel: 02-9398 5027; www.cyclehire.com.au). **Centennial Park Kiosk** is a lovely setting for a meal and a glass of wine. Beside it stands a charming, if curious, modern stone fountain.

The **Belvedere Amphitheatre** here provides an outdoor venue for events and productions. In summer, a popular Moonlight Cinema programme (www.moonlight.com.au) is held there. Films start at about 8.30pm, and tickets are available in advance from the website or at the gate from 7pm.

Kings Cross and Paddington

East of the Domain is the district of **Woolloomooloo** – a wonderful word, the origins of which cause some debate, but either mean 'place of plenty' or refer to a young black kangaroo. Woolloomooloo was threatened by demolition in the 1970s, but was saved by resident protests and union 'green bans'.

East of Woolloomooloo, bright lights and shady characters exist side by side in Kings Cross, just one railway stop from Martin Place. 'The Cross', is Sydney's version of Pigalle, in Paris, or London's Soho – neon-filled, a bit tacky but rather fun, crawling with hedonists of all persuasions. Action continues 24 hours a day, with a diverting cavalcade of humanity – the brightly coloured, the bizarre, the stoned, the happy and the drunk. On weekends, tourists flock to The Cross to glimpse a bit of weirdness. Sometimes though, the weirdest characters they spot are other tourists.

The main drag here is **Darlinghurst Road**, bohemian verging on sleazy and dotted with strip joints, fast-food outlets, tattoo parlours and X-rated book and video shops, backpacker hostels and cheap hotels. Gentrification is progressing rapidly, however, and several stylish bars, restaurants and hotels have opened. The neighbouring area of Potts Point offers good eating – try Fratelli Paradiso just off Macleay Street.

A five-minute walk (and a world away) from Kings Cross Station brings you to **Elizabeth Bay House** (www.sydneylivingmuseums.com. au; Fri–Sun 10am–4pm), a superb example of colonial architecture, built in 1835 and nestled in the posh enclave of Elizabeth Bay.

To the southeast of Kings Cross is **Paddington**, where the bohemian atmosphere and intricate wrought-ironwork (known as Sydney

Paddington Markets

Sydney's raucous Mardi Gras Parade

Lace) on the balconies of 19th-century terraced houses, remind many of New Orleans. After decades of dilapidation, it's now a fashionable, artsy place to live and one of Sydney's most sought-after suburbs, with house prices to match. 'Paddo', as the locals call it, offers plenty of good restaurants, antiques shops, art galleries, bookshops and trendy boutiques. One of the best markets in Sydney, **Paddington Markets** (www.paddingtonmarkets.com.au; Sat 10am–4pm) is held in the grounds of Paddington Uniting Church, 395 Oxford Street. It offers art and crafts and is enlivened by a variety of street entertainers.

Paddington's main thoroughfare, **Oxford Street**, which continues into the neighbouring suburb of **Darlinghurst**, is one of the hubs of Sydney's large gay community (others include Surry Hills, Newtown and Erskineville). The **Sydney Gay and Lesbian Mardi Gras** parade (www.mardigras.org.au), held here in late February/early March, has become a respected institution. The street is home to two good bookshops, Berkelouw and Ariel, and three of its more imaginative cinemas, the Chauvel, the Verona and the Palace Academy Twin.

Victoria Barracks is Oxford Street's renowned example of mid-19th-century military architecture, built by convicts to house a regiment of British soldiers and their families.

Around Sydney Harbour

Take a harbour cruise to appreciate hidden beaches, islets, mansions old and new, and even a couple of unsung bridges. Various companies run half-day and full-day excursions, or you can hop aboard a commuter ferry and get off wherever you like. If you're experienced, you could also rent a boat of your own and try weaving around the rest of the nautical traffic.

Fort Denison, situated on a small island, is graphically nicknamed 'Pinchgut'. Before the construction of a proper prison, the colony's more troublesome convicts were banished to the rock to subsist on a bread-and-water diet. In the middle of the 19th century the island was fortified to guard Sydney from the threat of a Russian military strike. Ironically, an attack finally came in World War II when an American warship, conducting target practice, hit old Pinchgut by mistake. You can visit Fort Denison, but only as part of a guided tour conducted by a national parks ranger (to book, tel: 1300072757).

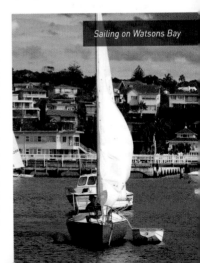
Sailing on Watsons Bay

Taronga Zoo (www.taronga.org.au; daily 9.30am–4.30pm; charge), a 12-minute ferry ride from Circular Quay, has an excellent collection of native and exotic animals in a superb setting. Over the heads of the giraffes you can see across the harbour to the sky-scrapers of Sydney. The zoo's Nocturnal House features indigenous night-time creatures illuminated in artificial moonlight, unaware of onlookers. The Rainforest Aviary houses hundreds of tropical birds. If you arrange your visit around feeding times, you can watch the keepers distribute food while they give talks about their charges.

For excellent views of the city and harbour, catch a ferry to **Cremorne Point**. A paved path winds from here along the shore of Mosman Bay to the ferry wharf, a distance that can be covered easily in about 90 minutes, from where you can catch a ferry back to Circular Quay.

Another popular ferry destination is **Watsons Bay** in the Eastern Suburbs. This suburb began as a small fishing community and it still retains a village-like atmosphere. Doyle's on the Beach seafood restaurant is located close to the ferry wharf, with wonderful harbour views. Nearby Camp Cove is a beach and picnic spot. A 30-minute walk from the beach along the foreshore leads to South Head, one of the headlands at the entrance to Sydney Harbour. The views are spectacular and the place gets packed each Boxing Day for the dramatic start of the Sydney to Hobart yacht race (www.rolexsydneyhobart.com).

Also accessible by ferry are **Kirribilli** – directly across the harbour from the city and also reached by foot over the Harbour Bridge – and **Balmain**, to the west of Circular Quay. Both places have lively café-and-restaurant strips and great harbour views from foreshore parks.

A quick trip from the city by bus or taxi is **Vaucluse House** (www.sydneylivingmuseums.com.au; Fri–Sun 10am–4pm, daily in Jan; charge). This splendid, 15-room mansion, begun in 1803, has its own beach, and comes complete with mock-Gothic turrets and battlements. A short walk away, down Coolong Road, is **Nielsen Park**, a bushland reserve that has a popular beach, as well as a café. There are good harbourside walks here too.

The golden sands of Bondi, Australia's best-known beach

Surf beaches

Further afield, both north and south of Sydney, are many kilometres of inviting beaches. **Manly** got its name when the first governor of the colony thought that the Aborigines sunning themselves on the beach looked manly. This pleasant resort, reached by ferry or Jetcat from Circular Quay, has back-to-back beaches – a sheltered harbour beach on one side, an ocean-facing surf beach on the other – which are linked by the Corso, a lively promenade full of restaurants and tables for picnickers.

Beyond Manly, beaches stretch all the way to Sydney's northern limits. Among these are **Curl Curl** and **Dee Why** (which offer good surfing), **Collaroy** and **Narrabeen** (with sea pools ideal for families), and **Newport, Avalon** and **Whale Beach** (a good spot for surfing).

At the northern tip of the Sydney beach region is **Palm Beach**, which is in a class of its own. The beautifully manicured gardens and villas for millionaires occupy the hills of the peninsula behind the beach. You can get to Palm Beach by taking the L90 bus from outside Wynyard railway station in the city centre; the trip takes about an hour.

Sydney Olympic Park

Bondi is a favourite with surfers and an Australian icon. The varied characters on the sand range from ancient sun worshippers to topless bathing beauties, and include quite a few pink British backpackers. Families tend to congregate at the northern end, where there is a wading pool. The beach gets very crowded on summer weekends. Set back from the beach, Bondi Pavilion has a café and bar, and is a good place for people-watching. Behind it is Bondi's main promenade and restaurant strip, Campbell Parade.

A string of lesser-known but lovely beaches stretch out to the south of Bondi, including Tamarama, Clovelly, Bronte and Coogee. These are best reached on foot by a scenic coastal walking track that starts at the southern end of Bondi beach. It takes about an hour to walk to Bronte; allow half an hour more for the Bronte to Coogee stretch. Buses run from Coogee to the city.

Olympic Sydney

Since the 2000 Games, Sydney's magnificent, purpose-built Olympic Park (www.sydneyolympicpark.com.au) has been used for a range of activities and around 5,000 events are now staged there each year. The best way to get there is to catch a Parramatta Rivercat ferry from Circular Quay; these depart hourly and provide a 50-minute scenic river trip before you alight at Olympic Park wharf.

The graceful, parabola-shaped centrepiece of Olympic Park, **ANZ Stadium** (www.anzstadium.com.au; guided tours from 11am), was Sydney's premier Olympic venue; it now hosts football games of all codes, from rugby league to soccer and Aussie rules, as well as cricket games, and also stages the occasional concert.

Not far away is **Sydney Olympic Park Aquatic Centre** (www. aquaticcentre.com.au; Mon–Fri 5am–9pm, Sat–Sun 6am–7pm). Besides its pools, the centre has five spas, a river ride, spray jets, spurting 'volcanoes' and a water slide.

Surrounding these and other venues are extensive parklands, good for gentle walks and picnics. There is also a small number of cafés and restaurants.

EXCURSIONS FROM SYDNEY

Within striking distance of Sydney – by car, train, or sightseeing bus – a diverse choice of destinations shows the variety of attractions offered by New South Wales. Trips to any of these places will deepen your understanding of Australia and its culture.

GOING WEST

A 90-minute trip west of Sydney by road brings you to the **Blue Mountains ❷**, a dramatic region of forested ravines and pristine bushland that is World Heritage listed. The Blue Mountains offer a wealth of adventure activities, art and craft galleries, and romantic escapes in grand country lodges or cosy bed and breakfasts.

The name derives from the mountains' distinctive blue haze, produced by eucalyptus oil evaporating from millions of gum trees. Well-marked walking trails criss-cross Blue Mountains National Park, passing streams and waterfalls, descending into cool, impressive gorges, and snaking around sheer cliffs. This breath-taking environment is easily reached from Sydney, either by road or on a two-hour rail journey. Trains run there several times daily from Central Station.

The region's best-known rock formation is the **Three Sisters**, a trio of pinnacles best viewed from **Katoomba**, the largest of 26 mountain towns. The **Scenic Railway**, the world's steepest passenger-carrying railway, descends from the cliff-top at Katoomba into the **Jamison Valley**. You can walk down a series of steps by the Three Sisters, stroll along a cool and refreshing trail and catch the Katoomba Scenic Rail to the top. Above, the **Scenic Skyway** carries passengers along a cableway 206 metres (675ft) above the valley floor. The **Scenic Cableway** descends over 500 metres (1,600ft) into the Jamison Valley.

For a less touristy view of the Blue Mountains, drive to the look-out at Govetts Leap, near **Blackheath**, 12km (7.5 miles) west of

The vast Jamison Valley lies below the Three Sisters

Katoomba. The panorama is magnificent.

Of the numerous walking trails in the Blue Mountains, many involve a steep descent into a valley and a steep climb back to the top. For information about walks in the area, see www.national parks.nsw.gov.au.

For more than a century, spelunkers, hikers and ordinary tourists have admired the **Jenolan Caves**, at the end of a long, steep drive down the mountains west of

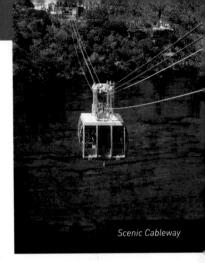

Scenic Cableway

Katoomba. Guided tours (tel: 1300 763 311; www.jenolancaves.org. au; daily 9am–5pm; charge) through the spooky but awesome limestone caverns last about an hour and a half. The atmosphere inside the caves is cool in summer, warm in winter, and always damp.

HEADING NORTH

Just north of Sydney is **Ku-ring-gai Chase National Park**. This area of unspoiled forests, cliffs and heathland fringing the Hawkesbury River, is home to numerous species of animals and birds. There are also many good walking trails through untouched bushland. West Head Lookout, on top of a headland, gives outstanding views of the river and ocean. The Aborigines who lived in this area long before the foundation of New South Wales left hundreds of rock carvings – mostly pictures of animals and supernatural beings. The information centre at Bobbin Head Road, Mount Colah (tel: 02-9472 8949) has maps pinpointing the locations of the most interesting carvings, as well as showing the park's network of trails.

THE HUNTER

Australia is one of the world's major wine-producing countries. The Hunter Valley, a two-hour drive north from Sydney, is the premier wine-growing area of New South Wales. The Hunter's 120 or so wineries harvest grapes in February and March, and welcome visitors throughout the year. The gateway to the Pokolbin region, where the majority of the Lower Hunter Valley wineries are located, is **Cessnock**, 195km (121 miles) north of Sydney. The tourist information centre, in the nearby town of Pokolbin, supplies touring maps and brochures, or you can join a day tour from Sydney.

Most of the Hunter wineries are open for cellar-door tastings. Some of the major establishments include Tyrell's, Lindemans, Wyndham Estate, Rosemount Estate, the Rothbury Estate and the McWilliams Estate.

Newcastle, the commercial centre of The Hunter, is located approximately 170km (106 miles) to the north of Sydney. It's a

Close to Sydney, the Hunter Valley is a lush, wine-growing region in New South Wales

coalmining and shipbuilding centre, and also offers well-developed recreational activities on the Pacific, the **Hunter River** and **Lake Macquarie**, the largest saltwater lake in Australia, very popular with weekend sailors and fishermen from near and far.

Further north, **Port Stephens** offers safe swimming beaches, a range of water activities and good fishing. Its bay is home to dozens of bottlenose dolphins, which can be viewed up close on a cruise.

Remote Lord Howe Island, home to some fabulous scenery

In the far north of New South Wales, 790km (490 miles) from Sydney, **Byron Bay** provides wonderful beaches and great surf. Whale-watching boat trips offer an opportunity to see humpback whales when they migrate along the coast here in June–July and September–October. The town is a haven for alternative lifestylers and millionaires.

LORD HOWE ISLAND

In the South Pacific, 600km (360 miles) east of Port Macquarie, Lord Howe Island is the world's most southerly coral isle. The snorkelling and scuba diving is splendid here, but non-swimmers can go out in a glass-bottom boat. There are also numerous walking trails, many birds and some unique vegetation.

Forests, beaches, mountains and all, Lord Howe Island only amounts to a speck in the ocean – around 1,300 hectares (3,220 acres) – with a population of about 350 and a couple of cars.

Bicycles and motorbikes are ideal for getting around as the roads are very quiet. You can fly out from Sydney or Brisbane in a couple of hours.

HEADING SOUTH

Thanks to a bit of historical gerrymandering, **Jervis Bay**, 200km (124 miles) south of Sydney, and 260km (161 miles) northeast of Canberra, is not actually part of New South Wales, but a separate Commonwealth territory, like the Australian Capital Territory. New South Wales surrendered the area to Canberra in the early 20th century, in case the future capital ever needed a seaport. The coastal enclave today includes an uncommon combination of facilities: inviting dunes and beaches rub shoulders with the Royal Australian Naval College, a missile range and Booderee National Park. Jervis, named after an English admiral, is correctly pronounced 'Jarvis', although locals are starting to rhyme it with nervous. The sand on Jervis Bay beaches is dazzling white and the sea is crystal clear. Dolphin Watch Cruises (tel: 02-4441 6311; www.dolphinwatch.com.au) operate from the town of **Huskisson** – sometimes you get to see migratory whales as well as dolphins. Not far away, a delightful glade called **Greenpatch**, in Booderee National Park, offers some remarkably tame wildlife, including kangaroos, wallabies and multicoloured birds.

For more beautiful beaches and tame wildlife, head 95km (60 miles) south from Huskisson to idyllic **Murramarang National Park**, just before the town of Batemans Bay. There are cabins and camping grounds here, as well as walking trails.

THE SNOWY MOUNTAINS

If you've come to Australia in search of snow, you need go no further than the southeastern corner of New South Wales. Skiing in the **Snowy Mountains** ❸ (known as the 'Snowies') is usually restricted to July, August and September. But even in the antipodean spring a few drifts of snow remain to frame the wild flowers of the Australian Alps. At the top of this world is **Mt Kosciuszko**, at 2,230 metres (7,308ft), named after an 18th-century Polish patriot by a 19th-century Polish explorer. This is the birthplace of three important rivers, the Murray, the Murrumbidgee and the Snowy.

Kosciuszko National Park is made up of approximately 6,700 sq km (2,600 sq miles) of the kind of alpine wilderness you won't see anywhere else: buttercups and eucalyptus and snow, all together in the same breath-taking panorama. Numerous hiking trails make for beautiful summer walks, and outside of the white season you'll barely see anyone. Cars must be equipped with snow chains from 1 June to 10 October. However, even during the summer months the weather can change for the worse at very short notice, so be sure always to carry a warm, waterproof jacket. The best-known ski resorts in this area are **Thredbo** and **Perisher Valley**.

NEW SOUTH WALES OUTBACK

Although New South Wales is the most populous and productive state (in both manufacturing and farming), as it extends into the seemingly infinite expanse of the Australian Outback, the population becomes much more thinly spread across the hard brown earth.

Dubbo, a five-hour drive from Sydney, is the sort of place where the Old Gaol, meticulously restored, is a

Winter sports in the Snowies

prime attraction, gallows and all. Just out of town, the **Taronga Western Plains Zoo** (www.taronga.org.au/taronga-western-plains-zoo; daily 9am–4pm; charge) is Australia's premier open-range zoo – a cageless convention of koalas, dingoes and emus, plus giraffes, zebras and monkeys.

Lightning Ridge, in the back of beyond near the Queensland border, enjoys one of the most evocative of Outback names. Fortune hunters know it well as the home of the precious **black opal**. Tourists are treated to demonstrations of fossicking (recreational prospecting), and there are opportunities to shop for opals.

Bourke is a small town on the Darling River whose name has come to signify the loneliness of the Outback, where dusty tracks are the only link between distant hamlets. 'Back of Bourke' is an Australian expression for a place that is extremely remote. Bourke looks a lot bigger on the map than on the ground.

Broken Hill (population around 19,000) is about as far west as you can go in New South Wales, almost on the border with South Australia. It's so far west of Sydney, there's a half-hour time difference. The town is legendary for its mineral wealth – it has produced millions of tons of silver, lead and zinc. Tourists can visit the mines, either underground or on the top. The neatly laid-out town, with streets named after various minerals – Iodide, Kaolin, Talc – has become an artistic centre, with works by Outback painters on show in numerous galleries. Pro Hart, one of Australia's best-known and most prolific painters, was a long-time Broken Hill resident. The School of the Air and the Royal Flying Doctor Service – both Outback institutions – give a further taste of life in the back of beyond.

CANBERRA

When the new nation was proclaimed at the turn of the 20th century, the perennial power struggle between Sydney and Melbourne reached an awkward deadlock. Each of the cities offset its rival's

claim to be the national capital. So they carved out a site in the rolling bush 300km (185 miles) southwest of Sydney, and it soon began to sprout clean, white, official buildings, followed by millions of trees and shrubs. Out of conflict emerged a green and pleasant compromise, far from the pressures of the big cities. Where sheep had grazed, the young Commonwealth raised its flag. As compromises go, it was a winner.

DESIGNING THE CAPITAL

To design a model capital from scratch, Australia held an international competition. The prize was awarded in 1912 to the American architect Walter Burley Griffin. He had grand designs, but it took longer than anyone imagined to transfer his plan from the drawing board to reality, owing not only to the distractions of two world wars and the Depression, but also to a great deal of wrangling. Burley Griffin, a Chicagoan of the Frank Lloyd Wright school, put great emphasis on coherent connections between the settings and the buildings, and between the landscape and the cityscape. Canberra's complete creation story is told in the National Capital Exhibition (Commonwealth Park, Regatta Place; tel: 02-6272 2902; www.national capital.gov.au).

Canberra ❹, at the heart of the Australian Capital Territory, has a population of almost 400,000. Although the city is an educational and research centre, it is

The Australian Parliament House

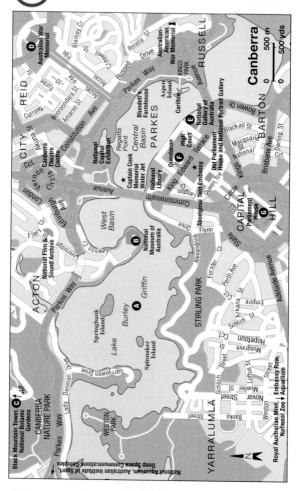

Canberra

0   500 m
0   500 yds

essentially a company town – and the local industry is government. The ministries are here, and the parliament with its politicians, lobbyists and hangers-on, and so are the foreign embassies. The Royal Military College Duntroon, Australia's first military college, founded in 1911, is based in Canberra, as is the Australian National University and the Australian Institute of Sport. In spite of this considerable enterprise, Australia's only sizeable inland city is both uncrowded and relaxed.

CITY SIGHTS

There are several good ways to see Canberra, but on foot isn't one of them; the distances are greater than you think. If you do want to walk, many of the main attractions are found near Lake Burley Griffin – but you'll still need three or four hours. It's a good idea to sign up for a bus tour; they come in half-day and all-day versions. Or take a City Sightseeing bus, which runs a 25km (15-mile) route stopping at all the main sights. You buy a 24-hour ticket, then hop on and off at will. Alternatively, you can drive yourself around the city or hire a bike, following itineraries that are mapped out in a free sightseeing pamphlet available from the Canberra and Region Visitors Centre (Regatta Point, Barrine Drive, Parkes; tel: 1300 554114; www.visitcanberra.com.au; 9am–5pm weekdays, till 4pm at weekends).

An effective starting place for a do-it-yourself tour is **Regatta Point**, which overlooks the man-made **Lake Burley Griffin Ⓐ**. Cleverly created in the middle of town, the lake – 35km (22 miles) around – is generously named after the town planner who realised the value of water for recreation as well as scenic beauty. You can enjoy fishing, sailing and windsurfing here, or hop on a sightseeing boat with Southern Cross Cruises (tel: 02-6273 1784; www.cscc.com.au; charge). Whooshing 147 metres (482ft) into the sky from the lake everyday, between 2pm and 4pm, the Captain James Cook Memorial is a giant **water jet** that honours the Yorkshireman's landing on Australia's East Coast in 1770. The **National Carillon**, another monument rising from Lake Burley Griffin (actually from a small island), was a gift from the British government. Apart from concert recitals, it tells the time every 15 minutes, taking its tune from London's Big Ben.

In a prime position at the tip of the Acton Peninsula is the excellent **National Museum of Australia** Ⓑ (www.nma.gov.au; daily 9am–5pm; free), a social history museum with themed galleries relating to the land, the people and the nation. The First Australians Gallery looks unflinchingly at the plight of the Aboriginal people after Europeans arrived, from the early massacres to the 20th-century government policy of taking Aboriginal children from their parents (the 'Stolen Generations').

NORTH OF THE LAKE

To get the best view of Canberra and surrounds, drive to **Black Mountain**. There are free lookouts here, or you can pay for a 360-degree perspective by going up the **Black Mountain Tower** Ⓒ (tel: 02-6219 6120; www.telstratower.com.au; daily 9am–10pm; charge), which stands 195 metres (640ft) high. A viewing platform circles the structure towards the top, and the designers couldn't resist adding a café and a revolving (and expensive) restaurant.

On the eastern slopes of Black Mountain, the **National Botanic Gardens** (www.anbg.gov.au; daily 8.30am–5pm; free) are entirely devoted to Australian flora – the most comprehensive collection in the world. In spite of Canberra's mostly mild, dry climate, numerous rainforest specimens flourish under intensive care. Walter Burley Griffin was so fascinated by the native trees and plants of Australia that he included this place in his original plan.

The only part of the capital designed with pedestrians in mind is the area around the **Civic Centre**. The original business and shopping district opened in 1927 – by Canberra standards that's ancient history – and comes complete with symmetrical white colonnaded buildings in a mock-Spanish style. Nearby are modern shopping malls, the **Canberra Theatre Centre** on London Circuit, and a historic merry-go-round in Petrie Plaza.

A more conventionally styled dome covers the vast **Australian War Memorial**  (www.awm.gov.au; daily 10am–5pm; free), which is a sandstone shrine climaxing a ceremonial avenue called Anzac Parade. There are war memorials all over Australia, but this is the definitive one, with walls poignantly inscribed with the names of more than 100,000 Australian war dead. Beyond the statues and murals, the memorial is the most-visited museum in Australia. Items displayed in its 20 galleries include uniforms, battle maps, and plenty of hardware, from rifles to a World War II Lancaster bomber.

Australian War Memorial

Closer to the lake is one final military monument: the 11-metre (36ft) tall **Australian-American War Memorial**, a slim aluminium shaft supporting a stylised eagle. It was paid for by public contributions to acknowledge US participation in the defence of Australia during World War II.

SOUTH OF THE LAKE

The mostly windowless walls of the **National Gallery of Australia**  (Parkes Place; tel: 02 6240 6411; www.nga.gov.au; daily 10am–5pm; free except for special exhibitions) were designed to enclose 'a museum of international significance,' as official policy decreed.

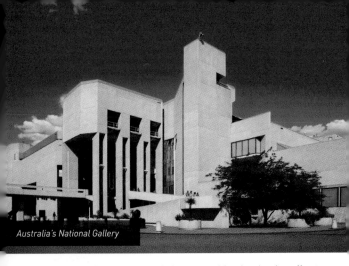
Australia's National Gallery

The enterprise has succeeded on several levels, showing off artists as varied as Monet and Matisse, Pollock and de Kooning, along with an honour roll of Australian masters, including Tom Roberts, Arthur Streeton, Sidney Nolan, Arthur Boyd and Albert Tucker. Further indications of the range of interests represented here are the displays of art from Pacific island peoples, Africa, Asia and pre-Columbian America. The gallery also plays host to touring international exhibitions.

A high point of the National Gallery is the collection of Australian Aboriginal art: intricate human and animal forms on bark from northern Australia, and deeply spiritual compositions of dots and whorls from the central deserts, which have evolved from ephemeral sand art to vivid polymer paint on board. The gallery also has a sculpture garden overlooking Lake Burley Griffin.

The **National Portrait Gallery** (King Edward Terrace, tel: 02 6102 7000; www.portrait.gov.au; daily 10am–5pm; free) sits alongside the National Gallery, in front of the High Court. It features portraits of prominent Australians.

One of Canberra's best kid-friendly attractions is **Questacon**, the **National Science and Technology Centre** ⊙ (King Edward Terrace; tel: 02-6270 2800; www.questacon.edu.au; daily 9am–5pm; charge), a hands-on science museum that is very much geared towards children and teenagers. There are more than 200 exhibits in seven galleries that explore the science behind sports and athletics, everyday technology and natural phenomena.

Also on the lakefront, the **National Library** (Parkes Place; tel: 02-6262 1111; www.nla.gov.au; Mon–Thur 9am–9pm, Fri–Sat 9am–5pm, Sun 1.30–5pm; free) houses more than 2 million books. This institution serves scholars and other libraries, and mounts exhibitions of rare books and maps. Its reading room houses an extensive selection of overseas newspapers and magazine publications. There are guided tours (free), a bookshop, and a café.

Canberra's **Old Parliament House** became the seat of government in 1927 and fulfilled that role until it was replaced in 1988. It is now the home of the **Museum of Australian Democracy** (King Edward Terrace; tel: 02-6270 8222; www.moadoph.gov.au; daily 10am–5pm; charge). Outside it is the **Aboriginal Tent Embassy**, a semi-permanent structure claiming to represent the rights of

⊙ WHAT'S IN A NAME?

The name of Australia's new capital city, derived from an Aboriginal word for 'meeting place', was officially chosen in 1913 from a huge outpouring of suggestions. Some of the more serious citizens wanted it to have a name as uplifting as Utopia or Shakespeare. Others devised classical constructions, for example Auralia and Austropolis. The most unusual proposal was a coinage designed to soothe every state capital: Sydmeladperbrisho. After that mouthful, the name Canberra came as a relief.

Australian Aborigines that has been around in one incarnation or another since 1972 (despite coming under attack several times).

A new parliament building to replace the old one was dedicated by Queen Elizabeth II in the bicentennial year, 1988. **Parliament House** G (tel: 02-6277 5399; www.aph.gov.au; Mon–Fri 9am–5pm; free guided tours) is worth a visit, its interior representing the best in Australian art and design. The Great Hall is dominated by a tapestry 20 metres (66ft) wide. The combination of an unusual design (partially underground), as well as exploding building costs, made the new complex a cause célèbre during its construction, especially when taxpayers noted the lavish offices, bars, swimming pool and a sauna.

Meanwhile, they're minting it in the southwestern district of Deakin, and you can take a look for yourself. The **Royal Australian Mint** (www.ramint.gov.au; Mon–Fri 8.30am–5pm, Sat–Sun 10am–4pm; free) has a visitors' gallery overlooking the production line where the country's coins are punched out. The factory also moonlights to produce the coinage of several other countries. The Mint's own museum contains coins and medals of special value.

Other Canberra attractions include the **National Film and Sound Archive** (www.nfsa.gov.au) and the **Australian Institute of Sport** (Leverrier Street, Bruce; tel: 02 6214 1010; www.auspot.gov.au/ais), where there are athlete-led guided tours of the Institute (daily at 10am, 11.30am, 1pm, 2.30pm).

OUT OF TOWN

Animal lovers don't have far to go for a close encounter with kangaroos, echidnas, wombats and koalas. The **National Zoo and Aquarium** (02-6287 8400; www.nationalzoo.com.au; daily 9am–5pm; charge) is only a few kilometres southeast of the city centre, in Yarralumla. You can walk through acrylic tunnels while sharks cruise past. The bird population includes parrots, kookaburras, cockatoos and emus.

The **Tidbinbilla Nature Reserve** (tel: 02-6205 1233; www.tidbin billa.com.au; daily 9am–6pm, 9am–8pm in summer), 40km (25 miles) southwest of Canberra, is a much bigger affair – thousands of hectares of bushland where kangaroos, wallabies and koalas flourish. Next to this unspoilt wilderness, the **Canberra Deep Space Communication Complex** (tel: 02-6201 7880; www.cdscc.nasa.gov; daily 9am–5pm), one of only three deep-space tracking stations in the world, operates in conjunction with NASA, the US space agency. The Complex has several exhibitions on space exploration.

QUEENSLAND

Queensland provides just about everything that makes Australia so desirable, and then adds some spectacular exclusives. The sun-soaked state gives you the choice of flashy tourist resorts, remote outback towns, a modern metropolis, rainforest, desert or apple

Another day in Surfers Paradise

orchard. But the most amazing attraction of all is Queensland's off-shore wonderland – the longest coral reef in the world, the Great Barrier Reef.

Queensland was founded in 1824 as a colony for incorrigible convicts, the 'worst kind of felons', for whom not even the rigours of New South Wales were a sufficient deterrent. In an effort to quarantine criminality, free settlers were banned from an 80km (50-mile) radius of the penal settlement in what is now Brisbane. But adventurers, missionaries and hopeful immigrants couldn't be held back for long. Queensland's pastureland attracted many eager squatters, and in 1867 the state joined the great Australian gold rush with a find of its own. Prosperity for all seemed to be just around the corner.

Mining still contributes generously to Queensland's economy. Above ground, the land is kind to cattle and sheep, and produces warm-hearted crops like sugar, cotton, pineapples and bananas. But tourism is poised to become the biggest money-spinner, for Queensland is Australia's vacation state, welcoming tourists (domestic and international) to wild tropical adventurelands in the far north, and the glitter of the Gold Coast in the south. The busiest gateways to all of this are the state capital, Brisbane, and the port of Cairns, which has become one of Australia's most popular tourist destinations.

BRISBANE

As befits a subtropical city with palm trees and back-garden swimming pools, **Brisbane** ❺ has a pace so relaxed you'd hardly imagine its population is about 2.3 million. The skyscrapers, some quite audacious, have gone a long way towards overcoming the 'country-town' image, but enough of the old, elegant, low-slung buildings remain as a reminder of former days; some are wonderful filigreed Victorian monuments, some are done up in bright, defiant colours. As well as having its own attractions, the city is also a handy gateway to nearby tourist sites such as the Gold Coast and Fraser Island.

The towers of Brisbane line the river

In 1859, when Brisbane's population was all of 7,000, it became the capital of the newly proclaimed colony of Queensland. The colonial treasury contained only 7.5 pence, and within a couple of days even that was stolen. Old habits of the former penal colony seemed to die hard.

The capital's location, on a bend in the Brisbane River, has made some memorable floods possible over the years – such as in 2010–11, when 38 people were killed and parts of the city were declared a disaster zone – but it sets an attractive stage for Australia's third-largest city. Spanned by a network of bridges (the first dated 1930), the river continues through the suburbs to the beaches and islands of Moreton Bay, 29km (18 miles) from central Brisbane. Some of Australia's most celebrated types of seafood come from here, notably the gargantuan local mud crabs and the Moreton Bay bug. Despite its unappealing name, this creature, related to the lobster, is a gourmet's joy.

Up the hill, on Wickham Terrace, stands an unusual historic building, the **Old Windmill** – also known as the Old Observatory – built

Queen Street shopping

by convicts in 1829. Design problems foiled the idea behind the windmill, which was to grind the colony's grain, and the energy of the wind had to be replaced by a convict-powered treadmill.

The nearby **Roma Street Parkland** is a diverse area of waterfalls, lakes, misty crannies of tropical vegetation, and floral displays with their own ecosystem of insects and birds. It is said to be the world's largest urban subtropical garden.

King George Square, next to City Hall, and the nearby **Anzac Square**, are typical of the open spaces that make the Central Business District (CBD) welcoming and pedestrian-friendly. **Queen Street Mall** is flanked by bustling stores and interspersed with shady retreats and cafés. Here, on a fine day, visitors from cooler climes should take a seat to enjoy the warm sun and watch the passers-by. Or you can stroll along Albert Street, from King George Square to the City Botanic Gardens.

Where central Brisbane fits into the bend in the river, the **City Botanic Gardens** (open 24 hours) turn the peninsula green with countless species of Australian and exotic trees, plants and flowers. **Parliament House** (tours Mon–Fri 9am–4.15pm), built in the 19th century in Renaissance style, overlooks the gardens and is the headquarters of the state's legislative assembly.

Across the Goodwill footbridge from the Botanic Gardens, or Victoria Bridge from the centre of town (and also accessible by ferry), is one of the city's main focal points, **South Bank**, a precinct of parks, gardens, restaurants, cafés and many other attractions stretching along the southern bank of the river.

At its northern end is the **Queensland Cultural Centre**, which puts most of Brisbane's cultural eggs in one lavish, modern basket. The Centre includes the **Queensland Art Gallery** (www.qagoma.qld.gov.au; daily 10am–5pm, free), the **Gallery of Modern Art** (same hours and website as gallery; free), the **Queensland Museum** (www.southbank.qm.qld.gov.au; daily 9.30am–5pm; free) and its offshoot **Sciencentre** (same hours as museum; charge), an interactive science museum aimed at kids and teens. Here too is the **Queensland Performing Arts Centre** (www.qpac.com.au), with several performance spaces.

To the south of the Cultural Centre, and linked to it by a beautiful bougainvillea-clad arbour, are the **South Bank Parklands**. The attractions here include a market (Fri 5–10pm, Sat 10am–5pm, Sun 9am–5pm) and an artificial beach (**Streets Beach**). There is also a

Gallery of Modern Art

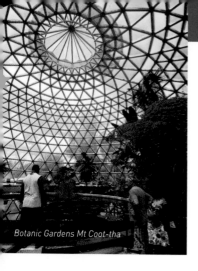
Botanic Gardens Mt Coot-tha

diverse array of restaurants, making this the place to head for on a sunny day, for an outdoor meal. Brisbane enjoys a reputation for chefs who make good use of their state's natural resources: mud crabs, avocados, macadamia nuts, mangoes, barramundi, coral trout and oysters, to name a few.

For a classic Brisbane pub, check out the **Breakfast Creek Hotel** (2 Kingsford Smith Drive; tel: 07-3262 5988; www.breakfastcreekhotel.com; daily 10am–2am), built in 1889, on the north side of a bend in the Brisbane River, about 5km (3 miles) east of the CBD. If you seek bars and restaurants, **Fortitude Valley**, just outside the CBD, is a lively precinct. Brunswick Street, the valley's main thoroughfare, is lined with nightclubs, street cafés, ethnic restaurants and arty little shops. This suburb is also the location of Brisbane's **Chinatown**. At weekends a market operates. Nightlife there can be fun, but it's wise to take a taxi when heading home after dark. Linking Fortitude Valley to Kangaroo Point is **Story Bridge**, a city landmark that you can climb with Story Bridge Adventure Climb (170 Main Street; tel: 1300 254 627; www.sbac.net.au; charge).

To escape the heat and rush of the city, try **Brisbane Botanic Gardens Mt Coot-tha** (daily 8am–5.30pm; free), in Toowong, 7km (4 miles) west of the city centre. Covering 52 hectares (128 acres), these are the largest tropical and subtropical gardens in Australia and feature a giant dome enclosing 200 species of tropical plants.

From here it's about 11km (7 miles) to **Lone Pine Koala Sanctuary** (www.koala.net; daily 9am–5pm; charge), one of the country's best-known collections of native animals. By boat from North Quay in the city centre, the trip is several kilometres longer, taking one and a half hours. The stars of the show, of course, are the koalas, mostly sleeping like babies, clinging to their eucalyptus branches.

The islands of Moreton Bay, some of which are unpopulated, make this a vast fishing and sailing paradise. **St Helena Island** (tel: 1300 438 787; www.sthelenaisland.com.au; charge), now a national park, became a penal settlement in the 1860s and remained a high-security prison until the 1930s; the excellent tours, which set out across the bay from Manly on the *Cat-O'-Nine Tails*, include a night-time ghost tour where actors re-enact scenes from the convict era. **Moreton Island** features **Mt Tempest**, at 285 metres (935ft) the world's highest stabilised coastal sand dune. On **North Stradbroke Island**, the Aboriginal community has developed a 90-minute tour called the **Goompi Trail** (tel: 0400 792 243; charge) where an Aboriginal guide explains the flora and fauna, with Dreamtime stories, bush tucker (food) and traditional medicine.

THE GOLD COAST

South of Brisbane, within day-trip distance if you're rushed, the **Gold Coast ❻** is a Down-Under version of Miami Beach. Although it may be overexploited (and best avoided during 'Schoolies' week in late November/early December, when Australia's high-school leavers celebrate

Koala mascot

The koala is Queensland's official emblem. Its only occupation is eating eucalyptus leaves, the odour of which impregnates its whole body, providing both antiseptic protection and a deterrent to predators.

their graduation with raucous partying) it's certainly dynamic, with lots of opportunities for recreation. And the beach – anything from 30–50km (19–30 miles) of it, depending on who's doing the measuring – is a winner. More than 20 Gold Coast surfing beaches, all patrolled by lifesavers, form the backdrop for activities such as swimming, sailing, boating, surfboarding and windsurfing.

The trip down the Pacific Highway south from Brisbane (78km/49 miles, roughly an hour's drive) is a study in Australian escapism. In the midst of forest and brushland grows a seemingly unending supply of amusement parks, luring fun-seekers with attractions for all the family; these diverting parks include **Dreamworld** (tel: 07-5588 1111; www.dreamworld.com.au; daily 10am–5pm; charge), **Sea World** (tel: 07-5588 2222 or 133386; seaworld.com.au; daily 9.30am–5pm; charge) and **Wet 'n' Wild** (tel: 13 33 86; wetnwild.com.au; daily 10am–5pm; charge). **Warner Bros Movie World** (tel: 07 5573 3666; www.movieworld.com.au; daily 9.30am–5pm; charge), one of the

Currumbin Wildlife Sanctuary

biggest, offers a Hollywood-style experience, including stunt shows, special effects and amusement rides. Other Gold Coast theme-park attractions include **Wet 'n' Wild**, which contains a giant wave pool, a white-water ride and a seven-storey speed slide. A terrible accident at Dreamworld that caused the deaths of four people in late 2016, on what was considered to be one of the tamer attractions, means that at the time of writing, many of the 'thrill rides' remain closed for safety audits.

Enjoying the surf on the Gold Coast

Nature-lovers can also enjoy **Currumbin Wildlife Sanctuary** (tel: 07-5534 1266; www.currumbin-sanctuary.org.au; daily 8am–5pm; charge), where masses of squawking rainbow lorikeets are fed each morning and evening. Other animals featured include koalas, kangaroos, Tasmanian devils, snakes and crocodiles. Currumbin is down towards the southern extremity of the Gold Coast, which ends at **Point Danger**. Beyond here lies New South Wales.

The essence of the Gold Coast is **Surfers Paradise**, as lively as any seaside resort in the world and much addicted to high-rise living. Here, when you're not sunbathing, swimming or surfing, you can go bungee jumping or just window-shop, eat out, socialise or wander through the malls, one of which, **Raptis Plaza**, is adorned by a full-scale replica of Michelangelo's *David*. The pace is hectic, and the revelry never stops. To unwind, take a leisurely boat cruise along the Southport Broadwater or the canals. Another Surfers Paradise landmark, not far from Sea World, is **Palazzo Versace**, the world's

Surfers Paradise

first Versace Hotel, billed as 'six star' and filled with all kinds of designer trappings.

Surfers Paradise is approached through a thicket of petrol stations, fast-food outlets and motels. Ahead you'll see a skyscrapered horizon of tall, slim apartment blocks interspersed with bungalows. The high-rise skyline of Surfers Paradise must now rank with Ipanema, Miami and Cannes for architectural overkill.

The lush green backdrop to the Gold Coast is known as the Hinterland. The area encompasses luxuriant subtropical rainforests, waterfalls and bushwalking tracks, mountain villages and guest houses, craft galleries and cosy farm-stay accommodation. **Lamington National Park**, a World Heritage area, is well worth visiting and is an easy day-trip from Surfers Paradise.

THE SUNSHINE COAST

For the sandy perfection of the Gold Coast with less commercialism (although they're working on it), try the resorts of the **Sunshine Coast ❼**, north of Brisbane. Some of Australia's best surfing is found here.

The resort closest to Brisbane, **Caloundra**, has a beach for every tide. The northernmost town on the Sunshine Coast, **Noosa**, used to be a sleepy little settlement, and the weekend haunt of local farmers and fishermen. That was in the 1960s, before the surfers, and the trendsetters from Sydney and Melbourne arrived, but it's still very laid back. **Noosa National Park**, a sanctuary of rainforest and under-populated beaches, occupies the dramatic headland that protects Laguna Bay from the sometimes squally South Pacific breezes. Fraser Island (see page 92) is easily reached from here.

This whole stretch is home to some of Queensland's most gorgeous coastline. Beaches such as those fronting the towns of **Maroochydore** and **Coolum** are gems.

The Sunshine Coast Hinterland is laden with plantations of sugar cane, bananas, pineapples and passion fruit. The area is also a centre of production of the prized macadamia nut. Above **Nambour**, the principal town of the Hinterland, is the Blackall Range, a remnant of ancient volcanic activity. Attractive Blackall towns such as **Montville** and **Maleny** offer crafts shops, cafés and tearooms.

To the south, just off the Bruce Highway near Beerwah, is **Australia Zoo** (tel: 07-5436 2000; www.australia zoo.com.au; daily 9am–5pm; charge). Made famous by the late Steve Irwin, the zoo has a wide variety of Australian wildlife, as well as many exotic species.

Noosa

THE GREAT BARRIER REEF

Australia's biggest and most wonderful sight, the **Great Barrier Reef ❽**, lies just below the ocean waves. Millions of minuscule coral polyps multiply and grow into an infinite variety of forms and colours here, to create the world's largest living phenomenon. The reef is home to at least 350 different types of coral. It stretches as far as you can see and beyond: more than 2,900km (1,430 miles) of submerged tropical gardens, sprinkled with hundreds of picture-perfect islands.

Observed more intimately through a diver's mask, the reef is the spectacle of a lifetime, like being inside a boundless tropical fish-bowl among the most lurid specimens ever conceived. Watch as a blazing blue-and-red fish darts into sight, pursuing a silver cloud of a thousand minnows; a sea urchin stalks past on its needles; a giant clam opens its convoluted, fleshy mouth as if sighing with nostalgia for its youth, a century ago.

Heading off to explore the reef

In 1770, James Cook was exploring Australia's east coast and literally stumbled upon the Great Barrier Reef when the *Endeavour* was gored by a lurking outcrop of coral. Patching the holes as best they could, the crew managed to sail across the barrier, and the vessel limped onto the beach at what is now Cooktown, where some major repairs had to be improvised.

The giant reef was proclaimed a marine park by the Australian Government in 1975, and placed on the World Heritage list in 1981, becoming the biggest World Heritage area in existence. It's now managed by the Great Barrier Reef Marine Park Authority (www.gbrmpa.gov.au), but is under threat from government-approved industrial activity within its boundaries, including dredging, ocean floor dumping and an increase in large tanker-ship traffic.

There are many ways of appreciating the reef, from glass-bottomed boats and semi-submarines, to a descent into an under-water observatory at the Townsville **Reef HQ** (see page 100), which claims the world's largest coral reef aquarium. Equipped with just a mask, fins and snorkel you can get close to the under-water world, or you can take the plunge and go scuba diving for the best encounters. If you're not a qualified diver you can take a crash course at many resorts. Organised excursions for advanced divers are also readily available.

In some places the coral stands exposed, but visitors are asked not to walk over it, as doing so severely damages the living organisms.

THE REEF ISLANDS

The reef – actually a formation of thousands of neighbouring clumps of reefs – runs close to shore in the north of Queensland but slants further out to sea as it extends southwards. Hundreds of islands are scattered across the protected waters between the coral barrier and the mainland. Several have been developed into resorts, ranging from spartan to sybaritic, but not all are on the reef itself. Following are some details about these resorts, heading from south to north:

Fraser Island is actually south of the Great Barrier Reef, but it's close enough and sufficiently interesting to rate inclusion here. About 120km (75 miles) long, Fraser is the largest sand island in the world, and a World Heritage site. Attractions include crystal-clear streams, lakes for swimming and rainforest trails. This is an unspoilt island for fishing, beachcombing and four-wheel-drive adventures, but not for sea swimming or coral dives (thanks to nasty rip tides and aggressive sharks). You can take excursions and flights to the island from Hervey Bay, or overnight at resorts, lodges, cabins or campsites.

Lady Elliot Island (www.ladyelliot.com.au) is a coral isle and part of the reef, but is situated south of the Tropic of Capricorn. Activities centre on diving, swimming and windsurfing. The gateway airport is in

Hamilton Island chapel

Bundaberg, a sugar-producing town 375km (233 miles) up the coast from Brisbane, and day-trip flights include use of the island's resort.

Heron Island (www.heron island.com), a small coral island right on the Great Barrier Reef, is heaven for divers. Nature-lovers can see giant green turtles, which waddle ashore between mid-October and March to bury their eggs in the sand. Heron Island also hosts thousands of migrating noddy terns and shearwaters. A resort on the island accommodates up to 250 people. There are no day trips and no camping.

Great Keppel Island (www.greatkeppel.com.au) is one of the larger resort islands, both in area and in tourist population (there's even a backpackers). The Great Barrier Reef is 70km (44 miles) away, but Great Keppel is surrounded by coral, and there's an underwater observatory. Its white beaches are among the best in the resort islands. Great Keppel is also one of the cheapest islands to reach from the mainland – a return ferry trip from Rosslyn Bay costs around A$55. For other angles on the island's treasures, rent a sailboard, catamaran, motorboat and/or snorkelling gear, or try water-skiing or parasailing.

Brampton Island (www.nprsr.qld.gov.au/parks/brampton-islands), is reached by sea from Mackay, however the resort has been closed for some years (rumours of a reopening are rife). With forested mountains and abundant wildlife, the island's mountainous interior is worth seeing, but access is hard unless you have your own boat. There's a small campsite on neighbouring Carlisle Island, which is uninhabited and connected to Brampton by a reef that is wade-able when the tide's out.

Island types

Not all of the reef's islands are made of coral. In fact, most of the popular resort islands are the tips of offshore mountains. True coral cays are smaller, flatter and more fragile.

For a taste of paradise try one of the Whitsunday Islands

Lindeman Island is the most southerly of the islands in the **Whitsunday Islands**  **archipelago**, which was named by James Cook after the feast of Pentecost, when he passed through. The Club Med Resort here closed down in 2012 – it has since been bought by a Chinese firm, who apparently mean to refurbish and reopen it (but at the time of writing, there was no real progress on the redevelopment of the resort)– but there's a basic Lindeman Islands National Park campsite. Several excellent walking trails cross the island, but access without your own boat is tricky.

With its jet airstrip, large marina, restaurants, bars and swimming pools, **Hamilton Island** (www.hamiltonisland.com.au) is the slickest international resort in the Coral Sea. There are hotel rooms, apartments and bungalows for almost all budgets. Away from the main resort is Qualia (tel: 07 4948 9222; www.qualia. com.au), aimed at the top end of the market. Wherever you stay, divers can go out to the reef by catamaran or helicopter. The island's rainbow lorikeets not only eat out of your hand but sit on your arm while they're doing it. There are tame kangaroos, too. You can fly to Hamilton Island from Sydney, Melbourne, Brisbane or Mackay, or fly to Proserpine and take a boat from Shute Harbour.

Long Island is 11km (7 miles) long – narrow and hilly with excellent beaches. Close to the mainland and far from the reef, it has the eco-friendly Palm Bay Resort (www.palmbayresort.com. au). Most of the island is national park and several trails lead through the rainforest.

South Molle Island also consists mainly of national park, plus a resort. South Molle is virtually joined to North Molle Island 2km (1.25 mile) away, and to the closer Mid Molle Island. The beaches are good (there are some quiet ones in the south), and you'll find nice trails for walks. The Great Barrier Reef is about 60km (37 miles) away, but coral reefs exist nearby.

Daydream Island is the tiniest of all the Barrier Reef resort islands, snoozing just offshore from busy Shute Harbour. Since beaches are not the island's strongest selling point, Daydream

☉ PERILS OF THE DEEP - AND THE SHALLOWS

Take care when you explore the Reef: some species of coral can cause very painful burns. The crown-of-thorns starfish may also be lying in camouflaged ambush for you, and it has thousands of poisonous spines.

But between December and April, the greatest threat of all comes from jellyfish ('stingers'). In summer these small, transparent, almost invisible creatures swarm along the north Queensland coast by the thousands – and their sting can be fatal. All the popular beaches have stinger net enclosures, along with vinegar for medication in case a tentacle gets through, but you should always heed the warning signs and, to be on the safe side, stay out of the water during the stinger season.

Island Resort and Spa (www.daydreamisland.com) has built swimming pools. The resort accommodates 300 guests plus day-trippers.

Hayman Island, the most northerly of the Whitsunday group, hosts the chic, international-class Hayman Island Resort (www.hayman.com.au), a lavish, five-star hotel. Hayman has a marina for drop-in yachts, and a choice of restaurants, bars and shops. The long, sandy beach suggests all sorts of watersports, organised for guests by the resort's activities staff. Some tiny, uninhabited isles are so close you can walk out to them at low tide. No day-trips to Hayman are available.

Magnetic Island is virtually a suburb of Townsville, the biggest city in northern Queensland. Many of the island's 2,500 or so permanent residents commute to work on the mainland by ferry. Being so easy to reach, it's a busy day-trip destination – by sea or helicopter – but Magnetic Island also has plenty of accommodation of all classes. Most of the island is a national park, busy with birds and other animals (including koalas in the eucalyptus trees), and the choice of beaches is enticing. Magnetic Island, 'Maggie' to the locals, was given its name by James Cook, whose compass malfunctioned here.

Famous visitors to **Orpheus Island** have included Zane Grey and Vivien Leigh half a century ago. Over 100 species of fish and 340 of the 350 known species of reef coral adorn underwater gardens in the island's several sheltered bays, with the channel at the southern point of Orpheus believed to host the reef's largest range of soft corals. The island is a national park, and Orpheus Island Resort (www.orpheus.com.au) is the sole resort. Nestling in a sheltered bay on the western (mainland) side of the island, the resort accommodates a maximum of 42 guests in 21 private rooms. Day-trippers and children under 15 are banned.

Hinchinbrook Island basks in a superlative of its own: 'The world's largest island national park'. A continental rather than coral island, but only 5km (3 miles) from the reef, Hinchinbrook has a couple of campsites (park rangers issue permits on the mainland) and a small resort with treetop bungalows. Inland from the smooth sand beaches, you will find mountains well worth climbing, as well as rainforest, waterfalls and bushland, where you'll come across wallabies. Day-trips depart from Cardwell.

Mulligan Falls in Hinchinbrook Island National Park

Bedarra Island, in the Family Islands group, has a very small, exclusive and pricey resort of just 16 villas (www.bedarra.com.au) on its west coast. The nearest mainland town is Tully, noted for having the highest average annual rainfall in the country.

Dunk Island, mostly national park, once had one of Queensland's best resorts, however this was destroyed by Cyclone Yasi in 2011 and is yet to reopen. You can still reach the island by boat from Mission Beach, and there are camping sites. Dunk offers a taste of genuine tropical rainforest. In the interior you can visit the carefully tended grave of Edmund Banfield, the island's first white resident. A journalist from Townsville, Banfield went to the island in 1898 to die quietly, having been given just weeks to live. He survived for 25 more years, writing books including *The Confessions of a Beachcomber* and *My Tropic Isle*.

Fitzroy Island, just 6km (4 miles) offshore, is easily reached on day excursions from Cairns. Fitzroy Island Resort (www.fitzroy island.com), the only accommodation on the island, reopened in 2010 after a complete refurbishment, and is a much glossier affair than it used to be. Fitzroy has reef around its shores and rainforest in the interior. There's a turtle rescue centre, a dive shop, good beaches and kayaks for hire.

Like Fitzroy, **Green Island**, one of the few resorts actually on the reef, is popular with day-trippers from Cairns, but when the crowds depart, the vacationers occupying the five-star Green Island Reef Resort (www.greenislandresort.com.au) have the tiny island, and its throngs of seabirds, to themselves. The Underwater Observatory, which claims to be the first of its kind in the world, lets you view the coral garden from the dry, some three fathoms below water level. In this situation, the fish come to look through the glass at the human beings in the tank. Another attraction, just a short walk inland from the ferry jetty, is Marineland Melanesia, which features crocodiles, stingrays, giant turtles, as well as Melanesian artefacts.

Lizard Island, a national park, situated about 30km (19 miles) off the tropical northern coast of Queensland, has rainforest, mangrove swamps and dozens of delectable beaches. The island is on the edge of one of Australia's most productive game-fishing zones, in which the half-ton black marlin is found, a favourite of the million-aires and celebrities who stay at the exclusive Lizard Island Resort (www.lizardisland.com.au). The only other alternative is at the other end of the price scale: a very basic campsite. The island is reached by air from Cairns.

THE TROPICAL COAST

The coast of mainland Queensland, which runs parallel to the Barrier Reef, terminates in the north with Cape York Peninsula, one of Australia's wildest and least populated areas. If you're heading there, it's best to go with an experienced operator – roads are often little more than dirt tracks. Following are a few highlights from further down in Tropical North Queensland, heading along the Capricorn Coast from south to north, starting just above Gladstone.

Rockhampton sits only a few kilometres north of the Tropic of Capricorn – 23°27' south of the Equator – the line that officially

Architecture in Rockhampton

divides the tropics from the subtropics. From here on northwards, you need no excuse to order an icy beer to assuage your tropical thirst. Rockhampton, known as the beef capital of Australia, has some genuinely interesting Victorian architecture, and is worth a walking tour. To the north, the Berserker Range offers spectacular limestone caves.

Mackay is the next substantial town, and even by Australian standards it's a long haul – about 340km (210 miles) along Highway 1, a road not noted for its scenery. Surrounded by dense fields of cane, Mackay processes one-third of the nation's sugar crop. At the harbour stands the world's biggest bulk sugar terminal. From July to December you can see cane crushing in progress at the **Farleigh Sugar Mill**, about 12km (7 miles) northwest of the town on the Bruce Highway. One of the largest parks in Queensland, **Eungella National Park**, lies inland from Mackay, in rugged mountain country. There are many walking tracks, ranging in difficulty from easy strolls to strenuous hikes. This is one of the few places in Australia where you can see platypuses in the wild. The best time is morning and late afternoon and there's a platypus viewing platform near the

Cairns

bridge in Eungella township. **Proserpine**, another sugar town, is situated inland from **Airlie Beach** and **Shute Harbour**, resorts from where there are boat trips to the Whitsunday Islands.

Another 265km (165 miles) closer to the Equator, you reach **Townsville** (population around 190,000), hub of the mining and cattle industries of Queensland's interior and a gateway for Magnetic Island (see page 96). In the historic town centre, along the river, are some photogenic old buildings with filigreed iron balconies and stately columns and arches.

One of Townsville's top attractions is **Reef HQ** (www.reefhq.com.au; daily 9.30am–5pm; charge), with a superb simulation of the Great Barrier Reef, an imax cinema, and a colossal aquarium. Right next door, the **Museum of Tropical Queensland** (www.mtq.qm.qld.gov.au; daily 9.30am–5pm; charge) combines maritime archaeology and the natural history of North Queensland. There's also a beachside playground along the 5-km (3-mile) **Strand**.

The landscape changes from dry to lush as you head north to **Cairns** ⑩, Australia's largest tropical city (population over 160,000).

A port laid out in grid style with huge blocks and extra-wide streets, Cairns has benefited economically from Australia's tourist boom and grown dramatically, but in the process has lost much of its former sleepy, tropical outpost atmosphere. In a prominent position on Trinity Inlet is **The Pier** (www.thepier.com.au), a shopping and leisure complex, which fronts a large marina from where reef cruises and game-fishing excursions depart. The centrepiece of the waterfront, called the **Esplanade**, is a huge landscaped swimming lagoon. A large shopping complex, **Cairns Central**, is located just past Shields Street.

Cairns makes an ideal base, within reach of the Great Barrier Reef, the World Heritage-listed Daintree rainforest, the temperate Atherton Tableland, the Outback and even Cape York. Hundreds of tour options are available, and the city has become a centre for adventure tourism. From hot-air balloon and bungee-jumping to skydiving and whitewater rafting, you can do it all here.

Cairns springs into action early in the morning, when speedy catamarans leave for Green Island and Fitzroy Island and smaller boats set sail with scuba divers or fishermen aboard. Travel agencies open their doors at 7.30am and keep going until after dark. They sell a large collection of excursions – to Green Island, inland to Kuranda and the Atherton Tableland, and up the coast to Port Douglas and beyond.

The town of **Kuranda**, 'the village in the rainforest', is a

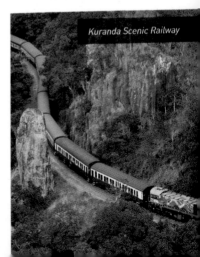

Kuranda Scenic Railway

short distance northwest of Cairns. It is very tourist-oriented, with numerous craft shops, galleries, restaurants and two markets (one held daily 9am–3pm, the other on Wed, Thur, Fri, and Sun 9am–3pm). Kuranda is linked to Cairns by two fascinating transport systems: the picturesque **Kuranda Scenic Railway** (tel: 07-4036 9333; www.ksr.com.au) and the **Skyrail Rainforest Cableway** (tel: 07-4038 5555; www.skyrail.com.au), which transports visitors to Kuranda in six-person aerial gondolas over dense, tangled rainforest. You can buy tickets for a round trip, taking the train one way and Skyrail the other. Skyrail riders can enter the forest on boardwalks at two stations on the way to explore the rainforest. A rainforest information and research centre is located at Barron Falls Station. The Skyrail experience is even better when it's misty or raining and the gondolas fill with a woody aroma as mists rise from below. Sweeping views of sugarcane plantations, the Coral Sea, beaches and offshore islands give way to eucalyptus forest and later to the huge fig trees, kauri pines and twisted vines of the 120-million-year-old rainforest.

The **Tjapukai Aboriginal Cultural Park** (www.tjapukai.com.au) at the base of Skyrail is home to the renowned Tjapukai Aboriginal Dance Theatre, which showcases the culture of the rainforest people of North Queensland. Performances, particularly at night, are primal and electrifying.

Beautiful coastal scenery is the reward along the highway north from Cairns to **Port Douglas**. The town's palm-fringed Four Mile Beach is most people's idea of a tropical paradise. Once a fishing village, Port Douglas has climbed on the tourism bandwagon, but it's more relaxed than Cairns. The **Sheraton Mirage Resort** is the flashiest hotel in town. Near it, Quicksilver (www.quicksilver-cruises.com) runs catamaran services to the islands and outer reef.

Popular destinations near Port Douglas are the sugar-milling town of **Mossman**, **Daintree National Park**, with its World Heritage-listed rainforests, and lovely **Cape Tribulation**, where, as the tourist

brochures say, 'the rainforest meets the sea'. There are also crocodile-spotting boat tours on the Daintree River. From Mossman north it's several hundred hot kilometres to the likeable river port of **Cooktown**, where James Cook's battered *Endeavour* was beached in 1770. The James Cook Memorial Museum tells all about it.

The tip of **Cape York Peninsula**, north of Cooktown, is a vast expanse of marshy terrain, prone to flooding, rife with crocodiles, and only negotiable in well-equipped four-wheel-drive vehicles driven by experienced people. The rivers are impassable from December to March; **Coen** is the largest town on the Cape.

NORTHERN TERRITORY

On the surface, the Northern Territory might seem an unpromising tourist destination. Its deserts, torrid tablelands, occasionally hell-like humidity and monsoonal woodlands may sound uninviting, but the wildlife is enchanting, the open spaces and big-sky scenery is magnificent and the people – though few and far between – welcome visitors with Outback hospitality and charm.

The population totals only around 244,000. Their median age is 30 years, the youngest of any Australian state or territory. About one in three Territorians identifies as an Aborigine, so cultural insights are part of the agenda for foreign visitors. This is the place to explore the grandeur, magic and mystery of Aboriginal beliefs, and to learn

The Ghan train

about the complex realities of modern life for the oldest surviving civilisation on Earth.

The Northern Territory covers about one-sixth of Australia's total area. Perhaps surprisingly, roads in the Territory are generally of a high standard and a four-wheel-drive vehicle is not necessary unless you specifically want to pursue off-road activities. The climate divides the land into two parts: the north, called 'the Top End', is lush, monsoonal, and very hot and humid. The rest of the Territory, known as the 'Red Centre', has drastically less rainfall and very hot, dry summers.

DARWIN

Australia's northernmost port, the capital of the Northern Territory, is a young, prosperous city radiating the optimism of the reborn, for **Darwin** ⓫ has survived more than its share of catastrophes. It was bombed in World War II, then after being rebuilt it was wiped out by Cyclone Tracy in 1974. Subsequently planners went back to the drawing board to design a bigger and better city.

With a population of 143,000, Darwin blends more than 50 different ethnic groups, including a large Chinese community. This is reflected in the city's wide range of Asian eating-places, ranging from up-market restaurants to budget-priced food stalls at the **Mindil Beach Sunset Markets** (www.mindil.com.au; late Apr–late Oct, Thur 5–10pm, Sun 4–9pm).

Darwin's daytime temperature averages above 30°C (86°F) all year, and the humidity can be debilitating. But while transients wilt, the locals know how to withstand the tropical conditions. They dress lightly and casually – even businesspeople wear shorts to work – use air-conditioning and drink a record amount of beer to quench their thirst. Although elsewhere in Australia a stubby means a small bottle of beer, order one in Darwin and you get a 2-litre bottle – almost half a gallon. Empty beer cans often end up as raw construction material for a flotilla of fanciful boats that compete in Darwin's annual slapstick regatta.

Even local chauvinists will admit that Darwin, approximately 4,000km (2,500 miles) from Sydney and Perth, is 'a trifle isolated'. However, that certainly doesn't seem to deter eager newcomers arriving from all parts of the country – if anything, it adds to the appeal of this adventurous and exotic state.

CITY SIGHTS

Historic buildings are the last things you'd expect to find in a city wiped out by a modern cyclone, but visitors can tour restored 19th-century

The Ghan train

A leisurely way to get to Darwin is by the Ghan, one of Australia's great train trips. Run by Great Southern Railways (www.greatsouthernrail.com.au) from Adelaide, the Ghan travels twice a week (Sunday and Wednesday) to Darwin (48-hours, two-nights) via Alice Springs (24-hours, one night) and Katherine. It does the same route in reverse leaving Darwin on Wednesday and Saturday.

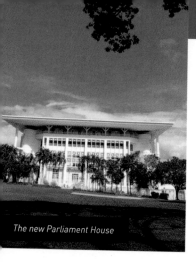
The new Parliament House

buildings that bring to mind the atmosphere of the pioneering days. The old **Government House**, overlooking the harbour, is an elegant example of colonial style (opened in 1883). Although a series of cyclones and the wartime bombs badly damaged the building (known as the Seven Gables), it has been put back together in fine form, and is surrounded by lovely tropical gardens. It replaced an earlier government building, which was eaten by termites, and in turn, it has been replaced as the regional seat of government by a new **Parliament House**, opened in 1994.

Dating from 1885, the stone building known as **Browns Mart** (www.brownsmart.com.au) is now a theatre. The building has a chequered past. Built as a miner's exchange, it was converted for use as a police station and subsequently served the community as a brothel.

Also on an offbeat historical theme, the **Fannie Bay Gaol Museum** (daily 10am–3pm) opened for business in 1883. Closed down in 1979, the jail allows visitors to follow the advance of penal progress since those early rough-and-ready days. The gallows were last used in 1952.

Other restored buildings include **Victoria Hotel** (built in 1894), and the former **Admiralty House** – now a restaurant, Char (www.chardarwin.com.au) – raised high on stilts in tropical style. A surviving portion of the old Anglican **Christ Church Cathedral** has been incorporated into the modern building.

At the harbour, the **Darwin Waterfront** (www.waterfront.nt.gov. au) precinct apartments, a convention centre, parks, a couple of swimming lagoons and a beach have been developed on former industrial land. Dozens of restaurants catering for all budgets have set up tables at the end of Stokes Hill Wharf. The precinct also houses the **Indo-Pacific Marine Exhibition** (www.indopacificmarine. com.au; daily in the Dry season 10am–4pm; charge), with live coral displays, and the **Australian Pearling Exhibition** (tel: 08-8999 6573).

Yachts and other pleasure boats dock on the western side of Darwin, at **Cullen Bay Marina**. Boats leave here for popular daily sunset cruises of Darwin Harbour. There are also shops, bars and restaurants.

Back in town, **Smith Street Mall** is a pedestrian-only shopping area, the retail heart of the city. The shady mall, with its stores, cafés and restaurants, is the perfect place for people watching. Nearby **Mitchell Street**, lined with bars, pubs, cafés, restaurants, hotels and motels, is the city's nightlife hub.

Walk along Bennett Street to Woods Street to see the **Chinese Temple**. Notwithstanding its sweeping roofs, the building is guaranteed cyclone-proof. It serves Buddhists, Taoists and Confucians.

The **Museum and Art Gallery of the Northern Territory** (tel: 08-8999 8264; Mon–Fri 9am–5pm, Sat–Sun 10am–5pm; free) at Fannie Bay is worth a visit for its Aboriginal art section and the exhibition commemorating Darwin's destruction by Cyclone Tracy on Christmas Eve 1974, which killed more than 50 people. Another popular exhibit is the stuffed body of 'Sweetheart', a 5-metre (16.5-ft) saltwater crocodile.

A building that looks remarkably ambitious for a town of Darwin's size is **SkyCity Darwin**, a gleaming white pyramid of a leisure and casino complex overlooking Mindil Beach. Here you can try your hand at two-up, the Australian game that's as simple as tossing two coins.

Lovers of tropical flowers will be delighted by the **George Brown Darwin Botanic Gardens**, 41 hectares (101 acres) of beautiful and

Feeding the crocs

exotic plants. In addition to the bougainvillea and frangipani, the orchids are a special source of pride.

Doctor's Gully Road, at the end of the Esplanade, is the site of a strange audience-participation ritual, the feeding of the fish. Tourists at **Aquascene** (tel: 08-8981 7837; www.aquascene.com. au) wade into the sea at high tide to hand-feed catfish, mullet, bream, milkfish and other sizeable denizens of the harbour.

Crocodylus Park (tel: 08-8922 4500; www.crocodyluspark.com; daily 9am–5pm; charge), a 15-minute drive east from the city centre, is home to around 1,000 crocodiles. The feeding sessions (at 10am, noon and 2pm) are impressive – time your visit to coincide with one.

SOUTH AND EAST OF DARWIN

About 120km (75 miles) south of Darwin, off the Stuart Highway, is **Litchfield National Park ⑫**, which covers around 1,500 sq km (580 sq miles) of tropical savannah wilderness. There are rocky escarpments, waterholes for swimming, waterfalls, patches of monsoon forest and various walking trails. Here, as in Kakadu National Park (see page 109), you can see '**magnetic anthills**', which are found scattered like tombstones in the bush. These are neither magnetic nor anthills – they're termite mounds, often taller than people, and are always aligned north–south, to achieve internal climate control.

Fogg Dam Conservation Reserve, 60km (37 miles) east of Darwin, off the Arnhem Highway, is a splendid sanctuary where a dozen species of water bird coexist on magical pools. A few kilometres further east you can take a **Jumping Crocodile Cruise** with Adelaide River Queen Cruises (tel: 08 8988 8144; www.jumping crocodilecruises.com.au; charge) on the Adelaide River and watch as crocodiles leap vertically from the water next to your cruise boat, attracted by chicken meat dangled over the side by crew members.

KAKADU NATIONAL PARK

Visitors – particularly birdwatchers and photographers – are unfailingly enthralled by **Kakadu National Park** ⓑ (www.kakadu.com.au; charge for non-NT residents over 16). The park covers 19,800 sq km (7,600 sq miles), and the accommodation and commercial centre is Jabiru, 250km (155 miles) southeast of Darwin. The scenery ranges from romantic to awesome. As an unparalleled outdoor museum of

Kakadu wetlands

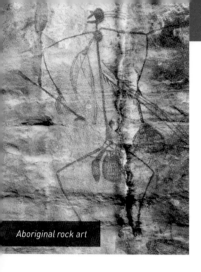

Aboriginal rock art

ancient Aboriginal art, the park is on the Unesco World Heritage List of places of 'outstanding universal value'. Some of the paintings have been here since the era of Europe's Palaeolithic cave art.

Nineteen different groups of Aboriginal peoples live between the Wild Man and East Alligator rivers. They lease the land to the National Parks and Wildlife Service and participate in the park's daily management, including working as park rangers.

Nature has neatly divided Kakadu into two worlds: the plains, with their lagoons and creeks, and the escarpment, a stark sandstone wall marking the western edge of Arnhem Land. From the top of the high plateau, waterfalls tumble to the lowlands in the wet season (November–March). The floodplains entertain water birds by the thousand. Their names alone are enticing enough to turn laymen into dedicated twitchers: white-throated grasswren, white-lined honeyeater and white-breasted whistler, to list but three of the species that breed in the park. The star of the show, though, is the jabiru, a stately variety of stork. In the mangroves you'll see striated herons, little kingfishers, broad-billed flycatchers and possibly also magpie geese, black shag, ibis and crested plover. A special delight is the sight of the delicately poised lotus bird, which seems miraculously to walk on the water. The waterways are rich in the eminently edible barramundi. Less appetisingly, the estuaries are home to the saltwater crocodile, a skilled predator that preys on barramundi, birds, small animals and, sometimes, human beings.

Kakadu's Rock Art

As many as 5,000 different sites, most notably at Nourlangie and Ubirr rocks, feature ancient Australian rock paintings in styles both primitive and eerily sophisticated. The earliest legacy consists of handprints and the imprints of objects that were dyed and thrown at cliff walls and cave ceilings for decorative effect. Many centuries later, abstract-expressionists in New York rediscovered a similar technique.

The next generation of prehistoric artists concentrated on depicting the figures of animals. Among them is a curious variety of anteater believed to have become extinct perhaps 18,000 years ago, a valuable clue to the age of some of these paintings. The same school of artists painted stick-figure humans in hunting and battle scenes using ochre pigments for colour.

Later artists introduced movement, such as hunters throwing boomerangs or spears. An innovation of this era was the employment of abstract marks around certain figures, like a modern cartoonist's squiggles representing a character's surprise or fear.

Thousands of years later, Aboriginal artists developed a remarkable style, now called X-ray painting. The profile of, say, a fish is clearly painted but instead of its scales we see its bones and internal organs, with the emphasis on edible or otherwise useful parts. After Australia was colonised, Europeans became a subject for the artists. There are pictures of British sailing ships and caricatures, scarcely flattering, of the new settlers holding recognisable muskets.

KATHERINE GORGE

The most spectacular natural attraction located at the Top End of the Northern Territory, **Katherine Gorge** is about 350km (217 miles) 'down the Track' from Darwin. The Track is the highway linking the Timor Sea and Alice Springs in the Red Centre of Australia; originally a rough path, fit only for bullock carts and camel trains,

Katherine Gorge

the route was upgraded by American servicemen during World War II to supply Darwin, which at the time was dangerously isolated and under Japanese attack.

Katherine, which is part of **Nitmiluk National Park** ⓮, is not a single gorge but a series of 13. In the wet season the torrents, waterfalls, whirlpools and rapids give an impression of thundering power. It is very hot and humid, and sometimes the rains cut off the roads, so is best visited in the dry season (April–October), when the water flows at a relative trickle. Flat-bottomed boats cruise along the river, mostly on the lower two canyons, where the water reflects sheer cliffsides, but more inquisitive travellers can explore the other 11 canyons upstream either by walking, hiring a canoe or swimming. The Visitor Information Centre in Katherine (tel: 08-8972 2650; www.visitkatherine.com.au) will book tours.

Among the sights are Aboriginal wall paintings portraying larger-than-life kangaroos and other native animals. Live kangaroos may be seen in the park, as well as echidnas and dingoes. Adding a tremor of excitement is the possibility of glimpsing a freshwater crocodile called Johnstone's crocodile. Unlike 'salties' which are rare visitors to the lower gorges, these fierce-looking reptiles are primarily fish-eaters and, fortunately, tourists do not figure on their menu. Bird life is colourful and includes hooded parrots and black cockatoos. Katherine is also home to a Savannah Guide Station (www.savannah-guides.com.au): the eco-accredited specialist guides focus on heritage, culture, and preservation of the environment.

ALICE SPRINGS

Traffic lights have slightly tamed the adventurous Outback atmosphere of **Alice Springs** ⑮, the biggest town in the Red Centre, 1,500km (930 miles) south of Darwin. 'The Alice' still looks rather like the frontier town you might imagine: a relaxed, friendly, slightly dishevelled community of pioneers, dreamers, transients and, more recently, throngs of tourists.

The Northern Territory's second biggest population centre has around 28,000 inhabitants. The desert climate can be extreme; in the summer it gets as hot as 42°C (108°F) and winter nights can drop below 0°C (32°F). Mercifully, the days and nights of spring and autumn are very pleasant, though the chances of seeing rain are slight. The Henley-on-Todd Regatta (www.henleyontodd.com. au), a whimsical fixture each August or September, is run on the sandy bed of the sometime Todd River, a wide wadi gullying through the centre of town. The boats are all bottomless, propelled by the racing legs of their crews.

Alice Springs first grew around a waterhole discovered in 1871 by the surveying party stringing the first telegraph line from Adelaide to Darwin – and from there to the rest of the world. Alice Springs was named after Alice Todd, the wife of South

Alice Springs from Anzac Hill

Aboriginal land

The Aboriginal Land Act of 1976 returned about one-third of the Northern Territory to its traditional owners. You need a permit to enter many areas, but not to drive through them on a public road.

Australia's postmaster general. He won a knighthood for pushing through the project; locally, the Todd River immortalises him.

Camel trains, led by Afghan cameleers, carried the equipment for the telegraph relay station built at Alice Springs and the supplies to keep the technicians alive. When termites devoured the first telegraph poles, replacements – heavy iron poles brought in from Britain – also had to be transported by camel train. Telegraphic messages aside, Alice Springs remained isolated until World War II – and until the 1960s it was little more than a crossroads market town. In February 2004, the Alice to Darwin 1,420-km (880-mile) railway extension was completed, fulfilling a century-old promise of a key economic and tourism link.

Like many Australian towns, Alice is bigger than you might expect, but the essential sights can be taken in on a walking tour. The main street, **Todd Mall**, is lined with galleries selling Aboriginal arts and crafts. Here, too, is the **John Flynn Memorial Church**, dedicated to the founder of the flying doctor service, and **Adelaide House Museum** (Mon–Sat 10am–4pm; free), the town's first hospital.

The **Todd Tavern** at the top of Todd Mall is the town's liveliest drinking spot. There's also an 'international standard' casino, **Lasseters**, on Barrett Drive.

The **Royal Flying Doctor Service**, which brings healthcare to the furthest cattle station, began in Alice Springs in 1928. You can visit the base and newly refurbished visitor centre (tel: 08-8958 8412; www.rfdsalicesprings.com.au; Mon–Sat 9–5, Sun 1–5pm; charge), on the south side of town. Opposite the RFDS is the **Alice Springs Reptile Centre** (tel: 08-8952 8900; www.reptilecentre.com.au; daily

9am–5pm; charge). Another unique service that makes Outback life slightly easier, the **School of the Air** is a radio, phone and internet link that links geographically isolated pupils across the country with each other and a teacher. You can see it in action at the Visitor Centre (www.assoa.nt.edu.au; Mon–Sat 8.30am–4.30pm, Sun 1.30–4.30pm; charge) on Head Street.

A couple of kilometres north of town, an unspoiled park surrounds the restored **Telegraph Station** (tel: 08-8952 3993 for information on guided tours). This was the most important relay station on the line; before the wires were strung a message could take three months to reach London from Adelaide. The relics here give a glimpse of 19th-century technology and the lonely life of the telegraph pioneers.

West of town, along Larapinta Drive, is the **Alice Springs Cultural Precinct** (Mon–Fri 10am–4pm, Sat–Sun 11am–4pm; charge), a group of museums and galleries. The **Araluen Arts Centre** (www.

Camel-riding basics

araluenartscentre.nt.gov.au; daily 10am–4pm; charge) has four art galleries featuring the works of Aboriginal artists of the Central Desert region. Also here is the **Museum of Central Australia**, (tel: 08-8951 1121, daily 10am–4.30pm) devoted to Central Australia's natural history, and the **Strehlow Centre**, displaying Aboriginal artefacts collected from the early to mid-20th century by anthropologist T.G.H. Strehlow, a researcher among the Arrernte people.

Located 3km (2 miles) out of town along Larapinta Drive is the **Alice Springs Desert Park** (www.alicespringsdesertpark.com. au; daily 7.30am–6pm; charge), renowned for its achievements in breeding rare and endangered species. A visit starts with a 20-minute film, then you tour walk-through enclosures and see the desert animals, which include emus, red kangaroos, reptiles and birds of prey.

If you wish to experience a camel tour, contact Uluru Camel Tours, located at the Ayers Rock Resort (www.ulurucameltours. com.au; tel: 08-8956 3333). In mid-July each year, the local Lions Club sponsors the **Imparja Camel Cup** – an exciting day of camel races at Blatherskite Park. The animals are launched from a kneeling start in a cloud of dust, and run just as fast as racehorses, though rather less gracefully.

A popular excursion from Alice concentrates on **Standley Chasm**, 50km (30 miles) to the west. This passage through the Mac-Donnell Ranges dwindles

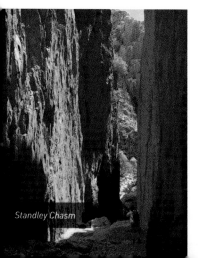

Standley Chasm

to the narrowest gap. The walls are so high and steep that the sun penetrates the bottom only fleetingly at midday. A few slender trees sprout from the rockface high above, reflected in the cool, still water of a natural pool at the far end of the gorge. During the wet season, from November to March, rain can suddenly flood the chasm.

A tourist drive called **The Red Centre Way** gives an incredible Outback experience. From Alice Springs, it heads through the western MacDonnell Ranges to Hermannsburg, a former Aboriginal mission, to **Kings Canyon** (in Watarrka National Park), and then on through the desert to **Yulara**, the site of Uluru (Ayers Rock). The trip covers about 1,200km (750 miles) and takes between three and five days. Much of the route is unsealed, so you will need a four-wheel drive vehicle. You will also need a permit to travel through Aboriginal land – for permits and information, contact the Tourism Central Australia Visitor Information Centre (tel: 1800 645 199; www.discovercentralaustralia.com).

ULURU (AYERS ROCK)

As the sun begins to set, crowds with their cameras gather by car and bus along 'Sunset Strip', the tongue-in-cheek name for a dusty stretch of car park. As the onlookers watch **Uluru** ⑯ (Ayers Rock; fee for a 3-day park pass) undergo its striking changes of colour, the mood is festive, friendly and relaxed. By coming here, visitors are fulfilling an Australian dream, getting to know this mystical 500-million-year-old rock that rises up from the red heart of the country.

The world's greatest rock, which seems like it dropped by divine design into the middle of nowhere, actually protrudes from a buried mountain range. At 348 metres (1,142ft) tall and some 8km (5 miles) around, it is even more impressive than the dimensions suggest. Standing alone in a landscape as flat as a floor, and tinted as bright as in your imagination, the monolith certainly lives up to its reputation. It's not hard to understand why the local Aborigines consider it to be a sacred place.

For the Aborigines it's not just a rock, it's a vital aspect of Dreamtime, encompassing the creation of the earth, linked with the life of the present and future. Aboriginal people have owned the rock under Australian law only since 1985. The local Anangu community leases it back to the government for use as a national park in return for a healthy income and participation in its management, but there is a caveat: the sacred places (signposted) around the base remain strictly out of bounds.

Tourists may climb Uluru on a defined path, but the practice is very much discouraged, as it has left a scar on the rock and deeply upsets the traditional owners. Some climbers have died during the experience and they are commemorated by plaques placed discreetly on the base of the rock. Park authorities close the climb if the temperature is over 36°C (97°F), if the track is wet, or if rain or high wind is forecast.

Uluru (Ayers Rock)

Since Uluru is the principle landmark in the region, there isn't much to see from the top anyway, and so a much better way to get to know the Rock is to circumnavigate its base on foot, either on your own (you won't get lost) or on a ranger-guided tour. Up close, the monolith reveals caves, dry rivulets, furrows, wounds and gashes, and what might be taken for fanciful engravings 60 metres (200ft) tall. Alternatively you can take a 30-minute scenic flight from Yulara or a day-trip by air from Alice Springs to get a bird's eye view of the rock and its surroundings.

From ground-level, the most inspiring views of the rock are to be seen at dawn and dusk. It's well worth getting up at 6am to stake out the mighty silhouette from 20km (12 miles) away, waiting for the sunrise. As first light strikes the lonely monolith it appears to catch fire, glowing red, then orange, finally seeming to emit rays of wondrous power. Only then the desert world comes to life: a hawk squawks, a rabbit rustles the brush, and hordes of pesky flies begin to buzz.

Only 36km (22 miles) by road west of Uluru, is another stupendous rock formation, **Kata Tjuta (The Olgas)** ⑰. From afar, Mt Olga and its satellites look like a scattering of dinosaur eggs or sleeping elephants, but they're actually higher than Uluru. Here, too, dawn and dusk colour the most fascinating views, the fantasy shapes changing with the hues and the movement of the shadows. You can get to know Kata Tjuta by a choice of hiking routes. The popular trail from the car park up to the lookout is officially described as 'suitable for family enjoyment', but it's steep and tricky enough to deter both the very youngest and oldest generations.

The path to Kata Tjuta: the name means 'many heads'

THE YULARA DEVELOPMENT

To cope with hundreds of thousands of visitors each year at Uluru, a comprehensive resort has been built in the township of **Yulara**. It could have been a disastrous blot on the landscape, but the Voyages **Ayers Rock Resort** (www.ayersrockresort. au) fits in discreetly, about 20km (12 miles) from the rock. The complex is low-slung and does not detract from the majesty of the surroundings.

Facilities range from campervan sites to a five-star hotel (with gardens, pool, spa, restaurants and bars and, of course, air-conditioning), right through to one of the finest glamping (glamorous camping) spots on Earth, Longitude 131° (http://longitude131.com. au). Here, visitors (including royalty) pay a large price for an exceptional view of the Rock from their beds, set in safari-style mega posh tents. The visitors' centre in the complex offers information, literature and audio-visual shows explaining the desert, the wildlife, geology, mythology and other angles to enhance your appreciation of the Red Centre.

Several airlines serve Yulara, and the views of the desert on the way are spellbinding. Otherwise you can take a bus or drive; it's about 450km (280 miles) by paved road from Alice Springs, a whole day in which to become acquainted with the desert in its many forms.

The best time of year to visit is between May and October, when the days are sunny and warm and the nights surprisingly chilly. In January, by contrast, the mean maximum temperature is 36.6°C (98°F) – not conducive to hiking.

SURVIVING THE OUTBACK

Three-quarters of Australia is desert – 'burning wastes of barren soil and sand', as the poet Henry Lawson described it. These vast empty spaces on the map hold an irresistible challenge for intrepid adventurers. Only vaguely comparable with desert of the Sahara type, the remote Outback supports vegetation – sometimes even luxuriant vegetation – and fascinating wildlife. But if you do want to venture off the surfaced roads and explore, there are a few precautions you must take.

Be prepared going into the Outback

Do not even consider driving into the Outback in the summer; the heat is unbearable. In the 1840s, explorer Charles Sturt recorded temperatures of 69°C (157°F) in the open and 56°C (132°F) in the shade.

Rain can also be a source of disaster; after many years of drought, a sudden deluge can transform the land into an enormous flood plain. Never camp in a dry riverbed.

Your vehicle should be a reliable four-wheel-drive, with a complete set of spare parts: two spare tyres and tyre repair kit, two spare tubes, coil, condenser, fan belt, radiator hoses and distributor points, a tin of radiator leak fixative, spark plugs, an extra jack (with a large baseplate to prevent sinking in sand or mud), snatch strap, 5 litres (a gallon) of engine oil, a pump, a tool-kit, an axe and a small shovel. Keep the petrol tank full and carry at least 20 litres (5 gallons) in reserve.

You will need to take reliable maps and be sure to plan your route in detail – and then stick to the plan relentlessly. At your point of departure, advise the police of your route, the estimated time of arrival at your destination, and the amount of rations you are carrying. Report to the police again when you arrive. Always seek local advice about the hazards you may encounter. If you wish to enter Aboriginal lands, you must first obtain permission, and at least four weeks' notice is required. Enquire at the government tourist office for the appropriate address (see page 245). In some areas you have to be equipped with a two-way radio or satellite phone.

Take adequate supplies. Most important is water – you will need 6 litres (1.5 gallons) per person per day, best carried in metal containers. Emergency rations should be made up of high-energy foods such as dried fruit, with canned meats, soup and fruit drinks. Some invaluable components of your first-aid kit will be aspirin, water-purifying tablets, salt tablets, diarrhoea pills, insect repellent, disinfectant, bandages and sun-block. Your personal survival kit, which you should carry with you at all times, must contain a compass, map, whistle, waterproof matches, pocket knife, bandage and adhesive plaster.

Other essentials include the following: a set of billycans (pails or pots with lids and wire bails), several sheets of heavy-duty plastic (2-metre/6ft square) and a length of rubber or plastic tubing.

A piece of nylon rope (30 metres/100ft long) may also come in handy.

Wear loose, light cotton clothing and a hat. Take warm clothing for nighttime. Space blankets can prove a boon: the shiny aluminium side turned towards the sun reflects heat away from the body, keeping the temperature normal. To keep warm, turn the shiny side inwards.

Do not drive at night. Kangaroos are a real hazard, and you may collide with cattle, camel and water buffalo, attracted to the roads at night because the surface retains warmth.

Be cautious

IN CASE OF CATASTROPHE

If your car breaks down, above all do not panic. Stay with your vehicle; it will be a welcome source of shade, and it is more easily spotted by aircraft than a person on their own. Do not risk searching for help during the day or night.

Make visible distress signals, using brightly coloured clothing or anything that contrasts with the earth.

Move around as little as possible, to conserve your body fluid. All your physical exertion should take place during the cool night hours.

Your main preoccupation must be water. It is important to ration your supply and set about collecting more by making a solar still, as follows: dig a hole about 1 metre (3ft) square and 50cm (20in) deep, away from any shade. Place a large billycan (pail or pot) in the bottom of the hole, and surround it with leafy foliage. Then cover the hole with a sheet of plastic and seal the edges completely with earth, making sure that the plastic does not touch the interior walls of the hole. If you have a length of rubber or plastic tubing, place it in the bottom of the billycan before you seal the edges of the sheeting, leaving the other end outside to act as a siphon. Place a small stone in the centre of the plastic sheet, right over the billycan. Moisture from the foliage will condense on the underside of the plastic sheet and will drip slowly into the billycan. In this way you will collect about 2 litres (0.5 gallons) of water per hole per day, so it's best to make several stills, at least 3 metres (10ft) apart. Change the position of the still every few days.

Small animals – frogs, lizards and snakes – are attracted to the stills and may provide an extra source of food. In principle, anything that walks, crawls, swims, flies or grows from the soil is edible, but beware of anything that has a bitter taste and of plants with a milky sap.

Another source of food and water in the northwest of Australia is the bottle-tree, which preserves water in its trunk for months after the wet season has ended. In an emergency you can also eat the rind of bottle-tree pods, chopped up and stirred with water.

WESTERN AUSTRALIA

When it comes to elbow room, the state of Western Australia has no competition. It's 10 times bigger than Great Britain, and covers more land than Texas and Alaska combined.

Most of the state's vast expanse is desert, semi-desert or otherwise difficult terrain. The bulk of the population of 2.6 million has therefore gravitated to the Mediterranean climate found around the beautiful capital city of Perth. Closer to Jakarta than to Sydney, Perth faces the Indian Ocean with an open, outward-looking stance. Here the cares of the big-population centres of eastern Australia seem a continent away – largely because they are.

The state's Outback produces great wealth, and even the forbidding deserts are bursting with minerals. It was gold that brought the state's first bonanza, during the 1880s and 1890s, followed by nickel, bauxite and iron. Considerably more appealing are the above-ground riches: the hardwood forests, the orchards, the vineyards and the springtime wild flowers. And, since the climate is so sunny, it's only fair that there is a beach for every possible mood along the 6,400km (4,000 miles) of coastline.

The first European to set eyes on a Western Australian beach (in 1616) was Dirk Hartog, a Dutch navigator making his way from

Western Australia

the Cape of Good Hope to Java. It was not long before other Dutch travellers touched base here, and one of them reported spotting a wallaby – he thought it was a giant cat with a pouch for its kitten. Later, in the 17th century, the British adventurer William Dampier sailed along the coast and happened upon an inlet he named Shark Bay, near Carnarvon. He could hardly wait to leave; the land seemed hopeless for farming, there was no drinking water, and he dismissed the indigenous population as 'brutes'.

More than 200 years after Hartog's 'discovery' of Western Australia, the British finally got around to colonising it. The site chosen, on the Swan River, became Perth. But what the Colonial Office considered a good idea turned out to be less brilliant in practice. It would take more than nice scenery and a temperate climate to attract settlers to what seemed, even by Australian standards, to be the end of the world. Problems of development persisted, including poor communications, financial difficulties

⊙ FROM COAST TO COAST

It takes just 4.5 hours to fly from the South Pacific to the Indian Ocean, from Sydney to Perth, but if you have 68 hours to spare, you can make the journey by train. The Indian-Pacific, a luxurious but not particularly rapid train operated by Great Southern Railways (www.greatsouthernrail.com.au), crosses the country twice a week in each direction. On its 4,352-km (2,702-mile) journey, it dissects the Nullarbor Plain, one section forming the world's longest stretch of straight track – 479km (298 miles) without a bend. There are numerous stops, but few towns, and none of any importance. In fact, there's not much to see – nothing but scrub, blue sky and telegraph poles for days on end – but passengers are well catered for with an observation lounge, a bar and even a music room.

Perth's skyscrapers

and a shortage of workers. Prospects for the new frontier became so precarious that the colony's leaders had to make an appeal to London, asking the government to send over a supply of forced labourers – convicts.

Even when these were forthcoming, nothing really worked in Western Australia until the gold rush during the 1890s, when the population quadrupled in just 10 years. Throughout the 20th century and up to the present, the exploitation of mineral deposits throughout the state has provided the main basis of its wealth – from uranium and iron ore to gas and oil. Once it was launched on the road to prosperity, there was no stopping Australia's largest state. Its isolation finally ended in the early years of the 20th century, when the transcontinental railway linked Perth and Sydney.

PERTH

Bright new high-rise office buildings scrape the clear blue skies of **Perth 18**. If this city, brimming with vigour and enthusiasm, were a person, you might imagine it had been born with the proverbial silver spoon in its mouth: a handsome, healthy, clean-cut youngster with every possible advantage, inevitably growing up to become an unqualified success in life.

Although history refutes the silver-spoon theory, you can't miss Perth's easy self-confidence. The people are relaxed, friendly and eager to help strangers. They are proud of their efficient town and its up-to-date facilities – the stylish shopping arcades, the art galleries and Entertainment Centre – and the great sailing, swimming, surfing and fishing right on its doorstep. The inhabitants won't fail to inform you that this tidy city sprawling magnificently along the looping Swan River is Australia's sunniest state capital.

Sunshine aside, Perth has called itself 'the city of lights' since the early days of the American manned space programme. As John Glenn, the first American to orbit the earth, passed over the city, middle-of-the-night Perth switched on every light bulb in town. It was a friendly gesture that brightened the lone astronaut's flight and put Perth's name in lights.

City sights

Few will get a chance to enjoy a spaceman's perspective, but the view over Perth from **King's Park Ⓐ** is a good compromise. These 400 hectares (990 acres) of natural woodland and wild flowers, manicured lawns and picnic sites, solemn monuments, bike tracks and lively playgrounds are found on the top of a bluff called **Mt Eliza**, right on the edge of the city centre. From here you look down on the wide Swan River as it meanders toward the sea, on the business district with its gleaming skyscrapers, and on the complexity of the well-landscaped municipal freeway system.

The **Swan River** was named after the indigenous black swans found here, first noted with amazement by the 17th-century Dutch navigator Willem de Vlaming. The river begins about 240km (150 miles) inland in the wheatlands of Western Australia. For most of its long journey, under the name of the Avon River, it is only seasonally navigable. But in Perth, with the Indian Ocean close enough to salt it, the Swan widens into a lake, and invites reflection – and attracts flotillas of yachts. By the riverside in the centre of town, the **Old Court House B** (Tue–Fri 10am–4pm; free) really is old, especially by local standards. Built in Georgian style in 1836, it's the oldest public building in Perth and houses the Francis Burt law museum.

Stirling Gardens, surrounding the courthouse, is a restful hideaway. The 'Ore Obelisk' monument here looks like a giant shish-kebab impaling all of the minerals mined in Western Australia; but don't expect to find gold or diamonds on the skewer – they don't seem to count.

Nearby, fronting the river, the Barrack Street Jetty, where ferries leave for Rottnest Island, is the site of the striking steel, glass and copper **Swan Bells Tower** (daily 10am–4pm; charge), completed in 2001. The 82.5-metre (270-ft) spire houses the 14th-century bells

of the church of St-Martin-in-the-Fields, London – a Bicentennial present from Queen Elizabeth II – which ring out every day except Wednesday and Friday, noon until 1pm. A top-floor observation deck gives views of the Perth skyline.

Indigenous black swan

The **Town Hall C**, at the corner of Hay and Barrack Streets, was built in the 1860s by convicts. If you look closely at the outline of the windows of the tower, you may perceive the design of broad arrows – the prison symbol that was stencilled on convict uniforms. Similarly Tudor in inspiration, but even less of an antique than the Town Hall, **London Court** is a 1930s shopping mall done up in 16th-century style. It fits in quite happily with the modern stores and interconnecting shopping precincts radiating from the **Hay Street Mall**, Perth's main shopping street. Cars are prohibited here, so the window-shopping is very relaxed.

A couple of blocks north, across Murray Street Mall, is **Forrest Place** on the corner of Wellington Street. Here, you'll find the **i City Visitor Information Booth** (tel: 08-9461 3444; www.visitperthcity. com; Mon–Thu 9am–4.30pm, Fri 9.30am–8pm, Sat 9.30am–4.30pm, Sun 11am–3.30pm).

In a city as young as Perth, with its skyline of tall, modern office buildings, those historic structures that have escaped the developer's demolition ball are proudly pointed out to visitors. **Government House D**, on St George's Terrace, Perth's main street, is the official residence of the Western Australia governor. Its Gothic effects date from the 1860s. Built by hard-working convicts, the house is used nowadays for state occasions and to accommodate visiting VIPs.

Heading west, St George's Terrace leads directly to the **Barracks Archway**, the last vestige of a headquarters building of the 1860s; this crenellated three-storey structure has been preserved as a memorial to the early colonists. Behind the

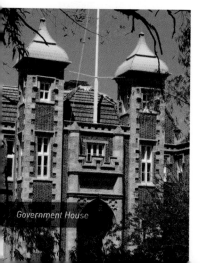

Government House

brick archway you can glimpse **Parliament House**, where the state legislature sits.

On the other side of the railway tracks (you can cross the unusual Horseshoe Bridge by foot or car) stands the **Perth Cultural Centre** E (www.perthculturalcentre.com.au) which was made up of the **Western Australia Museum** (www.museum.wa.gov.au), which is currently closed for the construction of a new museum, scheduled to open in 2020; the still-open **Art Gallery of Western Australia** (www.artgallery.wa.gov.au; daily 10am–5pm; free), the State Library; and the **Perth Institute of Contemporary Arts** (PICA; tel: 08 9228 6300; www.pica.org.au; Tue–Sun 10am–5pm; free). Part of the Western Australian Museum is the **Old Gaol**, which was constructed and used by convicts in 1856. The museum offers more than penal relics – there is also an extensive collection of Aboriginal rock paintings, head-dresses and weapons, and a 10-tonne meteorite. The Art Gallery of Western Australia displays paintings from several continents.

Also north of the city centre is the **Northbridge** district, which is full of lively ethnic restaurants, pubs and nightclubs, especially around James and Lake streets. If you're in the mood for gambling, head east for the **Crown Perth**, near the Causeway Bridge. Here, under one roof, you'll find a casino, a nightclub, restaurants, bars, theatres and hotels.

In the centre of town is the **Concert Hall**, the headquarters of the state's symphony orchestra. If you're looking for stage plays, the most atmospheric house is **His Majesty's Theatre** (825 Hay Street; tel: 8-9265 0900; www.ptt.wa.gov.au/venues/his-majesty-theatre), a plush Edwardian pile.

Well north of the centre, in the seaside suburb of Sorrento, the **Aquarium of Western Australia** (Hillary's Boat Harbour; 91 Southside Drive; tel: 08-9447 7500; www.aqwa.com.au; daily 10am–5pm; charge), an underwater-tunnel aquarium with interactive displays, offers whale-watching trips in season. For action entertainment, try the thrill rides at **Adventure World Theme Park** (179 Progress

Drive, Bibra Lake; tel: 08-9417 9666; www.adventureworld.net.au; Thur–Mon 10am–5pm, during school holidays daily 10am–5pm; charge), 15km (9 miles) south of the city.

TO THE COAST

It's only 19km (12 miles) down the river from Perth to the capital's Indian Ocean port, Fremantle – an enjoyable outing on one of the cruise boats that ply the Swan River. The river tours begin in the centre of Perth, at the **Barrack Street Jetty**. On the south side of the **Narrows Bridge**, note the **Old Mill** (Mill Point; tel: 08-9367 5788; Tue–Fri 10am–4pm, Sat–Sun 1pm–4pm), built in 1835, an imposing white windmill in the Dutch style from the first half of the 19th century. Perfectly restored, it's open for visits and tours.

Beyond this, on the opposite shore, just past Kings Park, spreads what looks like another transplant from Europe. The campus of the **University of Western Australia** was constructed and landscaped in a Mediterranean style, from the shrubs right up to the orange-tiled roofs. **Matilda Bay** harbours only a relative handful of the swarms of sailing boats that call the Swan River home. During World War II this was a base for Catalina flying boats. The bay is now the site of the Royal Perth Yacht Club.

The coastline of the Dalkeith district, near **Point Resolution**, is called Millionaires' Row, and the view of these fine mansions from the perspective of the river might evoke a dash of envy.

Freshwater Bay was named by the crew of HMS *Beagle*, the survey ship made famous by Charles Darwin. Beyond this bay, and a zigzag, the river tapers to a fairly narrow-gauge artery spanned by two bridges. Long-suffering convict labour built the first bridge at this site in 1866. It proved a boon to one of its creators, a celebrated outlaw named Moondyne Joe, an escape artist. The night before the ribbon-cutting ceremony, he broke out of Fremantle Prison and became the first person to cross the bridge over the Swan River, making a clean getaway.

Fremantle's quaint architecture

FREMANTLE

Although it's a serious international port, you'll remember the city of Fremantle for its casual charms. The town's special character combines Mediterranean-style sunniness with lovely Victorian quaintness and a down-to-earth demeanour.

For many years **Fremantle** ⑲ – 'Freo' to the Aussies – lay becalmed, a long way from tourist's eyes. Then came the America's Cup saga and suddenly Freo was saturated with world attention. New-found pride inspired the townsfolk in their sparkling campaign to restore the old terraced houses and other relics in time for the 1986–87 defence of the Cup.

Whether you think of Fremantle as a yachting base or a work-aday port, you'll want to see the sights of the harbour, where dream yachts, trawlers, ocean liners and cargo ships of every stripe rub shoulders.

Fremantle's highest point is **Monument Hill** in **War Memorial Park**. There are three memorials altogether, including one for the US personnel based in Fremantle who died in World War II. Another,

Old Fremantle Prison

an original periscope, commemorates the British and Allied submarine crews who perished in the same conflict. This is the place to watch the sun set over the Indian Ocean.

Back near the waterfront, and wasting an enviable view, the 12-sided **Round House** (tel: 08-9336 6897; www.fremantleroundhouse.com.au; daily 10.30am–3.30pm; free) looks like the forbidding, windowless prison it used to be. Actually, it's much more cheerful from the inside, with a sunny courtyard. Constructed in 1831, the Round House specialised in housing less serious criminals, although it was the site of the state's first hanging.

The more compelling penal complex is the **Old Fremantle Prison** (tel: 08-9336 9200; www.fremantleprison.com; guided tours daily 10am–5pm), convict-built in 1855 and continuously in operation as a maximum-security prison until the early 1990s. Since 1992 it has been one of Fremantle's most popular attractions; the fascinating guided tours leave every 30 minutes, and after-dark candlelit tours are also offered.

In pride of place on Victoria Quay is the **Western Australian Maritime Museum** (tel: 08-6552 7800; www.museum.wa.gov.au/maritime; daily 9.30am–5pm; charge), which highlights the state's maritime history. The **WA Shipwrecks Museum** (daily 9.30am–5pm; free) is housed separately, in the convict-built Commissariat building on Cliff Street. Here's a chance to see some notable wrecks such as the wooden hull of the *Batavia*, the flagship of the Dutch

East India Company, which went aground in 1629 and was salvaged and restored in the late 20th century.

The **Fremantle Arts Centre** (tel: 08-9432 9555; www.fac. org.au; daily 10am–5pm; free), at the other end of town, houses a gallery of contemporary art in a converted Victorian lunatic asylum, and stages concerts and other events.

Quokka Arms

The Rottnest Hotel (www.hotelrottnest.com. au), popularly known as the Quokka Arms, was built in 1864 and originally served as the summer residence of the governor of Western Australia.

If you're visiting Fremantle at the weekend, check out the lively **markets** (www.fremantlemarkets.com.au) held in a two-faced venue comprised of the Yard (Fri 8am–8pm, Sat–Sun 8am–6pm) and The Hall (Fri 9am–8pm, Sat–Sun 9am–6pm) sandwiched between Henderson Street Mall, South Terrace and William and Parry streets.

ROTTNEST ISLAND

Don't be put off by the name: there is nothing rotten in the state of Western Australia, and certainly not on Rottnest Island (www. rottnestisland.com), but even in translation, the name does the island no justice. Commodore Willem de Vlaming, who landed here in 1696, confused the indigenous quokkas (a species of small wallaby) with a species of rat, and called the island *Rottnest*, or 'rat's nest'. In spite of bequeathing the island this unkind and misleading moniker, the Dutch explorer considered Rottnest (rebranded 'Rotto' by Aussies) an earthly paradise. You may well agree.

A good reason for going over the sea to Rottnest (18km/11 miles from Fremantle) is to see the fetching little quokkas, bounding around with babies in their pouches, like their marsupial cousins. Other attractions are peacocks and pheasants, introduced when the governors of Western Australia used the island as a summer residence. And you can spot dozens of other species of wild birds, including osprey. Since 1941 the island has been a wildlife sanctuary, where it's forbidden to tamper with any of nature, even the snakes.

Rottnest is a quiet, idyllic, barefoot sort of island (except, perhaps, during 'Schoolies' week in late November/early December, when WA's high-school leavers celebrate their graduation with raucous partying). The number of cars is severely limited. Bikes are the most popular way of exploring the 40km (25 miles) of coastline. The snorkelling is amazing, as are the swimming, fishing and boating opportunities.

Two ferry operators serve Rottnest Island from Perth or Fremantle: Rottnest Express (tel: 1300 467688; www.rottnestexpress.com.au; departs from Fremantle and Barrack Street Jetty in Perth City) and Rottnest Fast Ferries (tel: 08-9246 1039; www.rottnestfastferries.com.au; departs from Hillary's Ferry Terminal in Sorrento). It's a 30-minute cruise from Fremantle and about double that from Perth. You can fly there in 20 minutes.

EXCURSIONS INLAND

Just to the east of Perth, the **Darling Range** is the beginning of a great inland plateau. Amid the tall trees and colourful wild flowers are lookout points with superb views of the city and the sea. Waterfalls, brooks and dams serve to refresh the relaxing scene.

The **Swan Valley**, only about half an hour's drive northeast of Perth, is a high-priority destination for wine lovers. The area is noted for its small, family-run vineyards. The wine-making tradition in the Swan Valley dates back to the foundation of Western Australia. If wine tasting and driving seem incompatible, you can take a coach tour of selected vineyards, or the popular river cruise with stops at one or two cellars.

Further east, the 150km (90-mile) green expanse of the **Avon Valley** provides pastureland for cattle and grows the grain to feed Perth and beyond. The colony's first inland settlement, **York** is proud of its history. More than a dozen 19th-century buildings, including an extravagantly designed Town Hall, have been restored; several now serve as museums. Just outside town, one of the early farms has been restored to a 'living museum' in which you can watch blacksmiths and wheelwrights at work. Clydesdale horses still plough the fields.

Yanchep National Park, 50km (30 miles) to the north of Perth, is known for its eucalyptus forests, wild flowers (in bloom in September) and a series of limestone caves. There is also an island-studded lake called **Loch McNess**, named after a local philanthropist, Sir Charles McNess. Don't bother looking for a Loch McNess monster. You can, however, see a koala colony here.

For those interested in wild flowers, the coastal town of **Geraldton**, 420km (260 miles) north of Perth, makes a good base for exploring the surrounding areas, such as Kalbarri National Park, where the flowers are at their best in August.

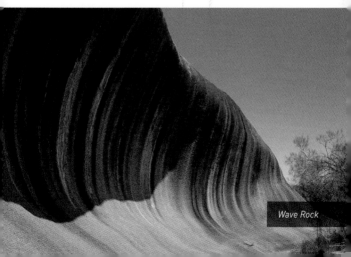

Wave Rock

NATURAL WONDERS

A feature reckoned to be more than 2.5 billion years old is **Wave Rock** (www.waverock.com.au), one of those natural phenomena worth a long detour – it's a 700km (437-mile) round trip by road from Perth. The rock stands near the small town of **Hyden**, about 350km (220 miles) inland from Perth, in the wide-open spaces where the wheat, oats and barley grow. The rock itself takes the form of a stupendous surfer's wave, as tall as a five-storey building, eternally on the verge of breaking. Walking under the impending splash is one of the state's most popular tourist activities. Other extraordinary rock formations in the area have expressive names like Hippo's Yawn and The Humps.

In **Nambung National Park** ⑳ about 250km (155 miles) north of Perth, the **Pinnacles Desert** is notable for myriad limestone pillars, jutting like stalagmites from the desert floor. Standing as high as 5–6 metres (16–20ft), the Pinnacles are scattered over perhaps

Pinnacles Desert

400 hectares (1,000 acres). When Dutch explorers first sighted the Pinnacles from their vessels in the 17th century, they thought they had found the ruins of a long-deserted city. In fact, they are entirely natural. Limestone formed around the roots of plants growing on stable dunes about 30,000 years ago. The plants died and the dunes moved on, leaving the calcified structures exposed. The park's entrance is located near the fishing village of Cervantes.

THE SOUTHWEST

Excursions to the southwestern corner of Western Australia encompass a delightful variety of scenery: beaches, vineyards, orchards, wild flowers (at their best in September) and forests of jarrah, karri and marri – eucalyptus species not found anywhere else. You can see some of these majestic trees – some up to 70 metres (230ft) high – in **Leeuwin-Naturaliste National Park**, just to the west of Margaret River (see page 139), and near **Pemberton**, about 140km (90 miles) south of the town of Margaret River.

Bunbury is a pleasant vacation town in the southwest, 180km (110 miles) from Perth; here you can swim with relatively tame dolphins at Koombana beach. The **Margaret River ㉑** region, between Cape Naturaliste and Cape Leeuwin, is honeycombed with limestone caves, some of which are open to the public. Near Yallingup, **Ngilgi Caves** (tel: 08-9755 2152; daily 9.30am–3.30pm; charge) form a fantastic underground world of elaborately carved limestone, and the tours are highly recommended.

Margaret River lies at the heart of the state's top wine-growing and gourmet-dining region. Specialities include brie-style cheese, fresh berries and marron (freshwater crayfish), while accommodation ranges from boutique guest-houses to five-star hotels or campsites. Places to stay include Cape Lodge, built with a South African influence. Margaret River township is the perfect spot from which to tour the region's noted vineyards, including Vasse Felix, Clairault, Sandalford, Leeuwin Estate, Xanadu and Cape

Mentelle. This area is also famed as one of the nation's best surfing locations. The closest beaches are at Prevelly, 10 minutes' drive from town.

THE GOLDFIELDS

Kalgoorlie ㉒, located around 550km (340 miles) east of Perth, retains the atmosphere of the anarchic gold-rush town it was in the 1890s. The streets, laid out in a grid, are wide enough for stagecoaches or camel trains to make a U-turn. It's like a Wild West movie set, with verandah-skirted saloons for every occasion. Optimists still scan old worked-over sites in search of forgotten nuggets – and the occasional whopper still turns up.

The first big strike of Kalgoorlie gold came in June 1893, when an Irishman named Patrick Hannan stumbled onto enough glitter to really kick up a fuss. A bronze statue of the bearded prospector has a place of honour in Kalgoorlie's main street, which bears his name.

When Hannan's news spread, thousands of prospectors rushed headlong into the goldfields. The almost total lack of water was the first desperate hardship they faced, and death from dehydration and disease took a heavy toll. The solution was found by another Irishman, an engineer named C.Y. O'Connor, who constructed a 560-km (350-mile) pipeline from a reservoir near Perth. You can still see the big above-ground pipes by the side of the road. Wounded by criticism of the project, O'Connor killed himself before the first drop of water reached Kalgoorlie.

As the prospectors came in from the surrounding desert with their sudden wealth, Kalgoorlie – and its neighbouring twin town of Boulder – turned into a rip-roaring supplier of wine, women and song. The pubs ran riot; many still retain their frontier atmosphere. Another old mining tradition is the red-light district of Hay Street, although apparently only three of the notorious 'tin-shack' brothels are still in business. You can gauge how prosperous the town was from the elegance of the Victorian buildings, most notably in the three-storey **Western Australia Museum, Kalgoorlie-Boulder** (daily 10am–3pm; free). This institution is stacked with exhibits detailing the life and work of those early prospectors.

Just north of Kalgoorlie, 5km (3 miles) along the Goldfields Highway, on the site of a disused mine, is the **Hannan's North Tourist Mine** (Sun–Fri 9am–4pm; charge), which highlights Australia's mining industry. There are gold panning demonstrations and former miners conduct underground tours.

A year before Paddy Hannan's big strike at Kalgoorlie, gold was discovered at **Coolgardie**, about 40km (25 miles) to the west. Today Coolgardie proudly bears the slogan of 'ghost town'. The historical markers here seem to far outnumber the population, which at the turn of the 20th century was 15,000 and now stands at only about 1000. Any good ghost town needs an interesting cemetery, and the inscriptions on the headstones in Coolgardie's graveyard tell revealing stories of the harsh frontier life. Among the Afghan camel drivers buried here, at least one is listed as having been murdered.

The Kimberley

THE KIMBERLEY

More than 1,500km (930 miles) north of the gold lode, one of the richest diamond mines in the world gives a sparkle to the rugged and remote **Kimberley** region of Western Australia.

The **Argyle mine** produces a sizeable heap of exquisite pink diamonds – a coveted rarity in the gem world – as well as vast quantities of industrial diamonds that are used for grinding and drilling. Huge machines, beside which humans look like Lilliputians, move the ore along to the Argyle processing plant, where millions of glittering carats are then yielded per year.

The Kimberley, a dramatic, elemental and spectacular area of waterfalls, thunderstorms, searing heat and torrential rain (the latter two depending on season), is thought to hide as many as half of all the diamonds on earth.

More than three times the size of England, the Kimberley has fewer people per square kilometre than almost anywhere else in the world. Some 30 percent of land is Aboriginal-owned and nearly half the population of nearly 40,000 are indigenous Australians.

The enormous region is particularly known for Aboriginal rock art, including the mysterious '**Bradshaw figures**', named after explorer Joseph Bradshaw, the first European to describe them. In 1891, Bradshaw wrote: 'The most remarkable fact in connection with these drawings is that wherever a profile face is shown, the features are of a most pronounced aquiline type, quite different from those of any native we encountered. Indeed, looking at some of the groups, one might almost think himself viewing the painted walls of an Egyptian temple.' The drawings are believed to have derived from an unknown culture that flourished some time before 15,000BC – long before the Egyptians had built their temples.

Wet and dry

Like all of Australia's tropical north, the Kimberley has two seasons: the Dry (April to October) and the Wet (November to March). Avoid the wet season. Not only is the humidity very high at this time, but torrential rainfall can rapidly turn rivers from mere trickles into raging torrents, flooding vast tracts of land. Many minor roads are closed for the entire wet season.

Until a few decades ago, the Kimberley was the domain of intrepid explorers. It has been opened up since, with tour operators using four-wheel-drive vehicles, boats, helicopters and small aircraft to reach the region's far-flung attractions: towering gorges on the Fitzroy River; **Purnululu (Bungle Bungle) National Park** with its orange-and-black beehive-striped mounds; the sandstone and volcanic country of **Prince Regent Nature Reserve**; the stunning gorge on the Fitzroy River of the **Geikie Gorge National Park**; the tidal 'waterfalls' near Derby; and the eerie **Wolfe Creek Meteorite National Park**. The Wolfe Creek crater was formed 300,000 years ago and is 850 metres (930yds) across, with a rim 50 metres (165ft) high. Aborigines call the area Kandimalal, which means 'the place

The extraordinary Purnululu National Park

where the snake emerged from the ground'. Europeans only discovered it in 1947. Its name was used for a disturbing Australian horror movie, *Wolf Creek*, released in 2005.

COASTAL ATTRACTIONS

On the coast, **Broome** ㉓ has a romantic past. It once supplied 80 percent of all the world's mother-of-pearl, when divers from Japan, Malaya and the Philippines went out on boats, diving for oysters and the pearls within them. The Asian aura is still prevalent, even though the mother-of-pearl business died with the introduction of cultured pearls and plastic buttons. Pearl farms do still operate, and you will find evidence of past glories in **Chinatown**, in the old Japanese boarding houses, and in the gambling and other pleasure palaces – all reminders of the port's early 20th-century heyday.

The main attraction today is **Cable Beach**, a fantastic 22km (14-mile) stretch of golden sands, so named when the underwater communication link between Broome and Java (and on to London) was established in the 19th century. At **Gantheaume Point**, low tide exposes dinosaur footprints about 130 million years old. If you stay late on the beach in March–April or August–September you may be lucky enough to see a natural phenomenon called 'the Staircase to the Moon', an illusion caused by the full moon reflecting on mud flats. It can be seen from the jetty at extreme low tides.

SOUTH AUSTRALIA

South Australia – like its official animal symbol, the hairy-nosed wombat – is pretty self-reliant and much more attractive than you may first think. Almost everything the state needs can be found within its borders: coal and gas under the desert, grain and cattle in the fields, fish from the Southern Ocean, and world-renowned wines from scenic vineyards. South Australia produces more wine than any Australian state, just under half of the nation's total.

The sights of South Australia are as many and varied as its resources: with the rugged grandeur of the Flinders Ranges, the sand dunes of the north, the green banks of the Murray River, and the surf of the Great Australian Bight.

The state's history is distinctive. There were no convicts – the colony was founded as a planned community run by wealthy idealists. The 'free settlers only' tag is a source of local pride. Sobriety and morality were keystones of the master plan, giving rise to a reputation for stuffy puritanism. Fortunately, the influence of the state's 'wowsers' (killjoys) has long faded. For example, Maslins Beach just outside Adelaide became Australia's first legal nudist beach (see page 157).

In some social respects, South Australia has led the rest of the country. It was first to grant votes to women, first to appoint an Aboriginal governor and first to appoint a woman governor. Spread across 1 million sq km (390,000 sq miles), the state occupies one-eighth of the entire continent, but because most of the state is unendurable desert, the inhabitants number only about one-thir-teenth of Australia's total population. More than three-quarters of these may be found living contentedly in the graceful capital city.

ADELAIDE

Adelaide ㉔ is easy to reach. Its international airport is efficient, land transport links are good and the city offers a cheerful intro-duction to Australia. Adelaide's sunny, dry climate beams on the city's many parks and gardens, as well as its elegant squares and broad boulevards.

With a population of over 1.3 million, Adelaide is a relatively sophisticated capital, where culture and good living are important elements of the local scene. There is a significant art gallery and the world's largest collection of Aboriginal artefacts in the South Australian Museum. The city puts on a world-acclaimed interna-tional festival of the arts every other year (even-numbered years)

⊙ FESTIVAL FRENZY

Sydney, Melbourne and Perth may all have their arts festivals, but none compares in size, prestige or sheer excitement to Adelaide's. Few cities in the world have such an extraordinary range of performance spaces, from the gleaming white Festival Centre to the outdoor amphitheatres and intimate lofts. The 'official' Adelaide Festival (www.adelaidefestival.com.au) lures the high-profile international acts, kicking off with free weekend concerts and firework displays in Rundle Park. The Fringe Festival (www.adelaidefringe.com.au), for less mainstream performers and artists, attracts thousands of acts from all over Australia, Europe and North America. Every spare corner of indoor space is devoted to some art exhibition, and every stretch outdoors to a site-specific installation.

Central Market

and a fringe festival annually. Founded by Peter Gabriel in 1982, the WOMADelaide (World of Music, Arts and Dance; www.womadelaide.com.au) festival takes place every February–March, and has an international flavour as well as an indigenous one.

Every day, the locals here pay tribute to international culinary art, dining out in hundreds of excellent restaurants. Chefs work with top quality raw material. You can see and taste it at the **Central Market** (www.adelaidecentralmarket.com.au; Tue 7am–5.30pm, Wed–Thur 9am–5.30pm, Fri 7am–9pm, Sat 7am–3pm) in Gouger Street, which features fresh produce from all parts of the state, including McLaren Vale olives, Coffin Bay oysters, Barossa mettwursts and Riverland dried fruits.

Nightlife encompasses concerts, theatres, clubs and a casino. The city has come a long way since the days when outsiders joked, 'I went to Adelaide once but it was closed.'

Adelaide was founded two generations after the settlement of Sydney, in the reign of King William IV, and named after his queen, the former Princess Adelaide of Saxe-Meiningen. Although the southern coastline had been well charted, the idea of building a city beside the Torrens River didn't catch on until the 1830s. Before the first earth was turned, the city was planned on paper, street by street and park by park. The business district covers the area of 2.6 sq km (1 sq mile). The model, with its built-in green belt, was a winner, and so it remains to this day.

City sights

The stateliest of streets in Adelaide is **North Terrace**, which delineates the northern edge of the business district and is lined with trees and distinguished buildings – mansions and museums, churches and memorials. Between the Terrace and the landscaped bank of the river is the **Adelaide Festival Centre** (www.adelaide festivalcentre.com.au), which calls to mind Sydney's Opera House, but with angular planes in place of billowing curves. Adelaide also managed to truncate Sydney's lavish price tag, but the relatively budget-priced $20-million complex still has a theatre for every occasion. The 2,000-seat Festival Theatre is convertible, in three hours, from an opera house to a concert hall with outstanding acoustics. A theatre for drama seats 600 people, an experimental theatre a further 400 and an outdoor amphitheatre another 1,000.

There are 90-minute backstage tours of the establishment (Tue and Thur 11am) and a theatre museum preserves South Australia's rich history and interest in the performing arts. Outside, bold sculptures are strewn around the plaza. You can eat outdoors in the Festival Centre's bistro overlooking the river, picnic on the lawn of the surrounding **Elder Park**, or take a sightseeing boat up the river to the **zoo** (www.adelaidezoo.com.au; daily 9.30am–5pm; charge), where you can pet the kangaroos and admire an outstanding collection of Australian birds, as well as many other international guests, both feathered and furry.

Behind the Festival Centre, **South Australian Parliament House** (www.parliament.sa.gov.au; guided tours on non-sitting days,

Mon–Fri 10am and 2pm) is dignified by 10 Corinthian columns and so much expensive stonework it enjoys the nickname 'marble palace'. The foundation was laid in 1881 but work continued, on and off, over the following 58 years. Across the road is **Government House**, the official residence of the Governor of South Australia.

Next door there's a startling change of pace: **Adelaide Skycity** (www.adelaidecasino.com.au) is a casino in a dazzling conversion of the old railway station. Just behind the State Library is the **Migration Museum** (Mon–Fri 10am–5pm; Sat–Sun 1pm–5pm; free), tracing the history of immigration.

Elsewhere along North Terrace, the **University of Adelaide** is at the heart of a cluster of cultural institutions. Whale skeletons fill the show windows of the excellent **South Australian Museum** (www.samuseum.sa.gov.au; daily 10am–5pm; free) as an alluring invitation. Inside is a monumental collection of Aboriginal artefacts. A large-screen video display relates the story of the Aboriginal Dreamtime hero Ngurunderi. Other countries are well represented in a comprehensive survey of ceremonial masks, shields and sculptures from South Pacific islands. And you can see a traditional trading vessel from New Guinea, with a bamboo deck and a sail made of bark.

The **Art Gallery of South Australia** (www.artgallery. sa.gov.au; daily 10am–5pm; free), which officially opened in 1881, covers many centuries of world art, ranging

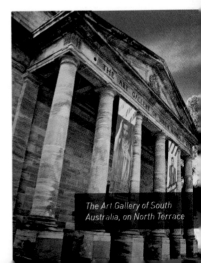

The Art Gallery of South Australia, on North Terrace

from ancient Chinese ceramics to contemporary Australian prints, drawings, paintings and sculptures. The gallery is also home to an extensive collection of Aboriginal art.

Two more historic buildings on North Terrace are **Holy Trinity Church**, the first Anglican church built in South Australia (begun in 1838), and **Ayers House** (tel: 08-8224 0666; www.ayershouse. com), a 45-room mansion furnished in an opulent 19th-century style. The house was owned by a local businessman and statesman, Sir Henry Ayers, after whom an admiring explorer named Ayers Rock. He was premier of South Australia seven times, and used Ayers House for state functions. Its ballroom, the hub of the Adelaide social scene, was regularly washed down with milk to make the floor fast and smooth.

To the north of Ayers House lie the **Botanic Gardens**, 20 hectares (50 acres) of lawns, trees, shrubs and lakes, with some exceptional botanical buildings as well, from the old Palm House brought from Germany in 1871 to the extraordinary Bicentennial Conservatory of 1988. The restaurant has an excellent reputation.

Bicentennial Conservatory

Parallel with North Terrace is **Rundle Mall** (www. rundlemall.com), an all-weather pedestrian mall, and the heart of Adelaide's shopping area. Its trademark is a sculpture comprising double-decked spheres of stainless steel reflecting the animation all around. The mall's merchants include department stores, boutiques, cafés and restaurants, all enlivened by street entertainers. The **Myer Centre** and the **Adelaide Central Plaza** are multi-storey shopping centres packed with speciality shops and the city's two department stores. Rundle Street (the eastern extension of Rundle Mall) is an arty and pleasant quarter, and contains Adelaide's two best pubs, the Exeter (www.theexeter.com.au) and the Austral (www.theaustral.com.au). The westward extension of Rundle Mall, Hindley Street, has clubs, live entertainment, amusement arcades and strip joints.

Located on Grenfell Street is **Tandanya** (www.tandanya.com.au; Mon–Sat 10am–3pm), an outstanding Aboriginal and Torres Strait Islander cultural centre showcasing art galleries, a workshop and performing arts. The shop offers authentic Aboriginal and Torres Strait Islander souvenirs.

North of the city centre, **Light's Vision** is not a sound-and-light show, as its name may suggest, it's a monument to the foresight of Lt-Col William Light, who was sent out in 1836 to find the ideal site for a model city, then devise the total plan for its development. Atop a pedestal on Montefiore Hill, his statue peers over the parklands, pointing at the city of Adelaide, which he created.

NEARBY PLACES

Adelaide has an outstanding public transport system, including the highly efficient O-Bahn, a 'bullet bus' that steers itself along its own smooth roadway at speeds of up to 100kmh (over 60mph). But nostalgia persists: the last surviving tramcars still clatter along between the edge of Victoria Square and the seashore at suburban **Glenelg**. This lively beach resort, from where a fishing pier forges far out to sea, was the original landing-place of the colonists who founded South Australia. A full-size replica of their vessel, a converted freighter named HMSs *Buffalo*, moored nearby, is now a restaurant. Also in Glenelg, in the historic town hall, is the **Bay Discovery Centre** (www.glenelgsa.com.au; daily 10am–5pm; admission free), dedicated to the social history and culture of the region.

Among other beaches near Adelaide, from north to south along the Gulf of St Vincent, you will find Semaphore, Grange, Henley Beach, West Beach, Somerton, Brighton and Seacliff.

South and east of the city, the **Adelaide Hills** provide a backdrop of forests, orchards and vineyards. There are pleasant drives, lovely walks, fine views, and plenty of picnic possibilities. The highest of the hills, Mt Lofty (770 metres/2,525ft) is only 15 minutes out of town by car, and features some good bushwalks. You can see wildlife at close range at **Cleland Wildlife Park** (www.clelandwildlife park.sa.gov.au; daily 9.30am–5pm; charge).

Hahndorf, a village situated 30km (19 miles) southeast of Adelaide, has changed little since it was settled in 1839 by German refugees. Many of the original buildings in this oldest surviving German settlement in Australia have been restored, and various folklore events brighten the tourist calendar, especially the Founders Day Festival, a marksmanship and beer-drinking celebration in January, and St Nicholas Night in December.

UP THE RIVER

The **Murray River** begins life in the Snowy Mountains in the Australian Alps, forms the frontier between Victoria and New South Wales, and enjoys its last meandering through the state of South Australia. It is the river that accounts for the beautiful vineyards, orchards and pastures along the way, not to mention the boating, fishing and water-skiing. In the 19th century the river was a main thoroughfare for both passengers and cargo, but the advent of railways and highways left the Murray more of a pleasure route.

Paddle steamers churn up nostalgia along the lower Murray, an hour's drive from Adelaide. Boats offer short excursions or voyages of several days. It's also possible to hire a houseboat and ply the river at your own pace, in which case you can fish for your own dinner. The Murray cod run to gargantuan sizes, and you can also catch 'yabbies', which are akin to crayfish.

THE BAROSSA VALLEY

Australia's best-known wine-producing region, the **Barossa Valley** ㉕, just 50km (30 miles) northeast of Adelaide, is also one of the prettiest. The scenery is beautiful: soft hills, sheep-grazing land, cosy villages and rows of vines that produce some famous wines – the 50 or so wineries produce about a quarter of Australia's total vintage. The valley is easy to explore: just 30km (19 miles) long by 14km (9 miles) wide. Accommodation ranges from luxurious colonial mansions to historic settlers' and miners' cottages, small motels and fully-serviced caravan and tent sites.

The Barossa was founded by German Lutherans who arrived in 1842, fleeing religious persecution at home. The Germanic atmosphere became a real liability when Australia entered World War I. Some of the Teutonic place names were changed for 'patriotic' reasons, and the government shut down a German printing house for fear that it would produce subversive leaflets.

Paddle boats on Murray River

Barossa vineyards

Nowadays, the valley's Germanic atmosphere is all part of the charm. You'll see neat stone cottages with filigreed verandahs and decorous gardens, and be able to taste bratwurst and sauerkraut to the accompaniment of oom-pah music.

The Barossa Valley is only about an hour's drive northeast of Adelaide, a perfect distance for an easy all-day excursion devoted to sniffing out the local colour and sampling the wines. There are guided tours (some departing from Adelaide) and cellar-door tastings. Be warned – the vineyard route is so popular that the roads and cellars can get crowded on Sundays and public holidays. Every alternate year (the odd numbers) the Barossa Valley stages an ebullient Vintage Festival (www.barossavintagefestival.com.au) in March or April, a week-long carnival as earthy as the wines it celebrates.

KANGAROO ISLAND

South Australia's favourite escapist resort, **Kangaroo Island** ㉖ is so big that you could spend a week finding the best places for swimming, fishing and sightseeing. Approximately 145km (90 miles) long and 30km (19 miles) wide, it's the country's third largest island, after Tasmania and the Northern Territory's Melville Island. For tourists in a typical rush, though, there are one-day excursions. It's only half an hour by air from Adelaide, but the most common route is by car ferry from Cape Jervis on the Fleurieu Peninsula (see page

156) to the settlement of Penneshaw across the rough Backstairs Passage (a 45-minute trip each way).

The English explorer Matthew Flinders, who circumnavigated Australia at the beginning of the 19th century, chanced upon Kangaroo Island in a storm. His hungry crew, amazed by the reception committee of fearless, friendly kangaroos, consigned some of them to the stew pot. Grateful for the sustenance, the great navigator named the place Kangaroo Island. Right behind the Flinders expedition came a French explorer called Nicolas Baudin. Despite having lost out to the British on his chance to claim the territory, he mapped much of the island's coastline and contributed some French names to its features. They are still on the map: places such as D'Estrees Bay, Cape Du Couëdic and Cape D'Estaing. In later years, settlers acknowledged Baudin's effort and built a

⊙ WHY 'KANGAROO'?

On one of his visits ashore, Captain James Cook asked a local what the strange leaping animal was. 'Kangaroo', came the reply. Cook passed on this intelligence to the whole world. An urban myth has it that the word *kangaroo* means 'I don't understand you' in an Aboriginal language; in fact, it comes from the word *gangurru*, meaning grey kangaroo.

There are around 45 species of kangaroos and wallabies, ranging in size from the red kangaroo, taller than a man, to the musky rat kangaroo, the size of a guinea-pig. Members of the family have adapted to many habitats: open plains, woodlands, rocky outcrops and cliffs – and some even climb trees. A young kangaroo, born in a near-embryonic state, crawls into its mother's pouch and attaches itself to a teat. It develops there for another four to eight months, depending on the species. Even when it is capable of venturing out it returns to the pouch between expeditions.

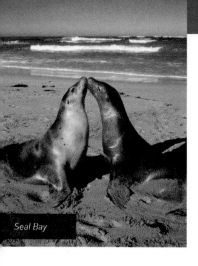
Seal Bay

white-domed monument to him at Hog Bay, called **Frenchman's Rock**.

The capital of Kangaroo Island, **Kingscote**, has a permanent population of around 1,700. Dolphins and seals can be seen frolicking just offshore, and there is a penguin colony nearby. The island is renowned for its unspoilt coastline of bays, cliffs and beaches. **Flinders Chase National Park**, South Australia's biggest nature reserve, takes up its western end. The animals there are wild, but in the absence of predators, the kangaroos, koalas and emus have become extroverts, often trying to sponge or steal food from visitors. On the south coast, **Seal Bay** belongs to Australian sea lions. They are so unafraid of humans that you can wander among them, guided by a national park ranger. Birdwatchers are thrilled by local species, which show clear differences from mainland relatives, and a noisy population of migratory birds from distant lands.

THREE PENINSULAS

Just to the south of Adelaide, the **Fleurieu Peninsula** is an easy-to-reach, easy-to-like vacationland of surfing beaches, vineyards and history. At the beginning of the 19th century, the French explorer Baudin named the peninsula after his navy minister, Count Pierre de Fleurieu. The first industry to be based on the peninsula was whaling, centred on **Victor Harbour**. It's now the area's biggest town, and a very popular year-round resort.

Yet another historic location is **Maslins Beach** on the Gulf St Vincent coast. Here, in 1975, a new leaf was turned in the evolution of Australian social customs. This was the nation's first legal nudist beach.

Further inland, scores of vineyards basking in the sunshine of the Southern Vales are the reason for the peninsula's fame. They've been making wine here since 1838, to great effect. Many of the wineries encourage wine drinkers to stop in and try the vintages. The best-known area of wine production is **McLaren Vale**.

The **Yorke Peninsula**, located to the west of Adelaide, first became important during the 19th century as a copper-mining district. The majority of the region's miners were drafted in from Cornwall, England, and their touch can still be seen in the design of the old cottages and churches in the area, and the baking of Cornish pasties. Museums and the ruins of the mine superstructures provide constant reminders of the peninsula's heyday, which continued until the 1920s.

The **Eyre Peninsula** encompasses beach resorts, wheat fields, bushland, industrial centres and a prized wilderness, the **Lincoln National Park**. Set atop magnificent cliffs at the tip of the peninsula, the park is home to kangaroos and birds as diverse as emus, parrots and sea eagles. Fishing boats big and small lay anchored in the attractive deepwater harbour of **Port Lincoln**, the tuna-fishing capital of Australia, and you can visit the home of the great white shark on a cruise to Dangerous Reef.

Port Lincoln celebrates **Tunarama Festival** (www.tunarama.net) on the foreshore of Boston Bay each January over Australia Day weekend (26 January). Highlights include the Tuna Tossing Championship, which sees world-class athletes turn up to throw large fish.

About an hour's drive west of Port Lincoln is **Coffin Bay National Park**, an unspoilt stretch of coast. Fishing and swimming are the main draws, and there are many isolated beaches and bays to explore.

The biggest city on the peninsula is **Whyalla**, which grew from a solid base of heavy industry – as heavy as iron and steel. If visiting a blast furnace is your idea of fun, join a tour of the local steelworks (tel: 08-8645 7900); you can also visit the iron ore-mining area.

The Eyre Peninsula reaches as far west as the small town of **Ceduna**, where the vast expanse of the **Nullarbor Plain** begins. It's more than 1,200km (745 miles) from Ceduna westward to the next town of any significance (Norseman, in Western Australia). Filling stations do occur, but the route is lonely and gruelling. Nullarbor is Latin for 'treeless', an indication that the plain is also waterless. But water is there if you know where to look for it: underground in limestone caverns. The highway follows the dunes and cliffs that lie along the length of the Great Australian Bight.

THE FLINDERS RANGES

For scenic splendour, South Australia's Outback competes well with the remote areas of the other states, nowhere more impressively than at the southern end of **Flinders Ranges National Park** ㉗,

Flinders Ranges

450km (280 miles) due north of Adelaide. Rising from a landscape as flat as the sea, the tinted peaks speak poetry to lovers of robust scenery. In the spring the rugged wooded hillsides come to life with a flood of wildflowers, but at any time of year the scene is intriguing. The mountains,

What's an opal?

Opal is not a crystal but more like quartz, made up of silica with a small amount of water. Unlike diamonds, opals are used only for jewellery.

like the desert, are much more colourful at close range.

An outstanding phenomenon found in the Flinders Ranges is a huge natural basin called **Wilpena Pound**. Rimmed by sheer cliffs, the saucer is approximately 20km (12 miles) long and 8km (5 miles) wide. Although it looks like a crater, it was actually formed by folding rocks. Wilpena Pound is not only spectacular as a scenic and a geological curiosity, it also wins admiring squawks from birdwatchers. This is a place where you can spot species including butcherbirds, wagtails, galahs, honeyeaters and wedge-tailed eagles.

The flat floor of the Pound is perfectly designed for bushwalks (suggested routes are signposted) – but not in summer, when it's too hot. In any season it's essential to carry drinking water. There's only one way into the amphitheatre, through a narrow gorge occupied in rainy times by Wilpena Creek.

An area of such grandeur was bound to inspire Aboriginal myths and art over thousands of years. Timeless rock paintings can be inspected near Wilpena at Arkaroo, and at Yourambulla Cave, south of the village of **Hawker**.

COOBER PEDY

The opal-mining town of **Coober Pedy** ㉘ must rate as one of the most bizarre tourist attractions in the world. When you say 'desert', this is what it means: in the summer the daytime temperature can

Opal quartz

reach 50°C (122°F) in the shade, supplies of which are extremely limited. In the winter the nights become unpleasantly cold. Yet nearly 3,500 people make their home in this far corner of the Outback.

At first glance, the town looks very much like a hard-hit battlefield. The almost treeless terrain consists of hundreds of mounds of upturned earth. But beneath the surface, things are not so bleak. The name Coober Pedy comes from an Aboriginal phrase meaning 'white fellow's hole', for the settlers have survived here by burrowing hobbit-like into the side of a low hill. The temperatures within are constant and comfortable, regardless of the excesses outside. Among the dug-outs are residences of some luxury, with electricity and wall-to-wall carpets. Also underground is a Roman Catholic chapel, plus several motels and B&Bs, a café, a restaurant, a bookshop, opal shops, museums and a pottery shop.

Regular tours by bus or plane bring the curious crowds to Coober Pedy, which is about 950km (590 miles) northwest of Adelaide. The tours visit underground homes as well as the local opal fields, where most of the world's opals are mined, with demonstrations of opal cutting and polishing. Having learned the intricacies, you can buy finished stones and jewellery on the spot. Or try noodling in the mullock heaps: all you need is a rake or a sieve to sift through the rubble at the top of each mineshaft, and if you're lucky you may find an overlooked gem. No permit is required for non-profit fossicking, although you must obtain the permission of the landholder first. Tours to Coober Pedy also explore the desert landscape outside town.

VICTORIA

By Australian standards, the state of Victoria is a midget. About the same size as Great Britain, it is the smallest state on the mainland, but its more than 5.9 million inhabitants give Victoria Australia's highest population density.

Over 70 percent of Victorians (4.5 million of them) live in the capital, Melbourne, a centre for finance, industry, culture and sport. The city folk live within easy striking distance of the state's bushland and 19th-century boomtowns, the sea, the vineyards and the ski slopes. Some of the scenery is so rich and pretty that the state's first name was Australia Felix – Latin for bountiful or lucky. For tourists, the state's relatively small size and varied landscapes make for convenient exploration.

Victoria was the earliest state to industrialise, but it's still a leading farming power as well – hence the nickname of 'Garden State'. This agricultural potential remained unexploited until the 1860s, after the state's gold rush fizzled out. Unemployed ex-prospectors eagerly fanned out as farmers, working land they had bought for £1 per acre. Immigrants in search of a figurative pot of gold followed in a steady flow that reached a tidal wave after World War II, with the policy of 'populate or perish'. This produced both curious ethnic pockets around the state and the cosmopolitan effervescence of a multicultural society within the dignified confines of the capital city.

MELBOURNE

Elegant parks and gardens splash green patterns across the map of **Melbourne** ㉙, softening the rigours of its precise grid plan, and offering merciful breathing space on the edges of the city centre's hubbub. This is a friendly city of serious buildings and imposing

Victorian architecture. Its air of distinction may have something to do with the fact that the city was founded not by prisoners (as was Sydney) but by adventurous free enterprisers with their own vision of success.

It's all so grand you might forget Melbourne's rough-and-tumble pioneering days. The gold rush broke out in Victoria in 1851, only a few months after the fever hit New South Wales. A gold strike at Ballarat so electrified the state that Melbourne itself risked becoming a ghost town; businessmen locked their offices or shops and rushed off to the goldfields, and gold-crazed crews abandoned their ships. New immigrants rushing in to fill the gap lived in shacks and tents. Successful diggers, on their return to Melbourne, had so much money to dispose of that morals loosened considerably.

Australia's two largest cities, Sydney and Melbourne, are fierce rivals. Sydneysiders blast Melbourne's climate; Melburnians ridicule Sydney's self-satisfaction and lack of culture. Whatever

☉ IT COULD HAVE BEEN BATMANIA

Australia's second city could have sounded so different if the Governor of New South Wales, Sir Richard Bourke, had not been a traditionalist. The first settlement of tents and huts on the Yarra had been called Bearbrass, for reasons that are not entirely clear. Yarra Yarra was also suggested as a possible name for the growing town, and so was Batmania, in honour of J. Batman, a settler from Tasmania who bought 40,000 hectares (100,000 acres) from the Aborigines. (The fact that he bought the territory, albeit at a derisory price, rather than simply stealing it, was a rare occurrence for the period.) But when Bourke visited the region in 1837, he decreed that the town should be named, in the customary fashion, after a British dignitary – in this case the Prime Minister, Lord Melbourne.

Happy Melburnians

Sydneysiders say about Melbourne's unpredictable weather, the southerners can point to several international surveys that rank their city higher than their northern rivals in terms of quality of life.

Melbourne is sport mad. 'Footy' – Australian Rules Football – is the main attraction here. Cricket is also a passion. Both are played at Melbourne Cricket Ground (the MCG), a focal point of the city's sporting and cultural life. And as for the horses, the Melbourne Cup is so all-engrossing that the first Tuesday in November, when the race is run, counts as a legal holiday.

In the last couple of decades of the 20th century, Melbourne was a city that emptied after dark, but all that has changed dramatically. Residents have moved back into the inner city, and the Central Business District now has cafés, bars and nightclubs. Melburnians have something of a reputation as gourmets and with some 3,000 restaurants in the city they are spoilt for choice.

City sights

A pleasant aspect of Melbourne can be viewed from the level of the **Yarra**, the river at the centre of the city. On the last few kilometres of its journey to the sea, the Yarra plays host to freighters, pleasure boats and rowing regattas. And it waters the gardens, reflects the skyscrapers and invites cyclists and joggers to follow its course along pretty paths. For a look at the skyline and a glimpse of river

Melbourne landscape from the Yarra

commerce, take one of the cruise boats that leave from **Princes Walk** by **Princes Bridge**.

Aerial views over the river and the city illustrate the ample hectares of green in the parks and gardens in among the business-like blocks. The best vantage point is the observation deck of **Eureka Skydeck 88** (inside the Eureka Tower; www.eurekaskydeck.com.au; daily 10am–10pm; charge), 285 metres (935ft) above **Southbank**, a riverside shopping and strolling precinct on the southern bank of the Yarra. The view extends beyond Westgate Bridge to the west, the Dandenong Ranges to the east and the shimmering expanse of Port Phillip Bay to the south. Those with a good head for heights can try **The Edge** (additional fee), a glass cube jutting out of the building, which gives those inside a feeling of hanging in mid-air.

Also at Southbank is the **Crown Entertainment Complex**, housing the 500-room Crown Towers Hotel and the Crown Casino, one of the country's largest gaming establishments.

Just past the Crown complex and the Melbourne Exhibition and Convention Centre is *Polly Woodside*, a square-rigged, 70-metre

(230ft), iron-hulled sailing barque, recalling the adventurous times of the last days of sail in the late 19th and early 20th centuries. Launched in Belfast in 1885, the restored ship is the centrepiece of the **Melbourne Maritime Museum** (tel: 03-9656 9804; www.polly woodside.com.au; Sat–Sun 10am–4pm, daily in school holidays; charge), which is run by the National Trust.

If you walk a little way downriver and cross over a footbridge, you'll find yourself in **Melbourne's Docklands** (you can also get here on a free City Circle tram from central Melbourne). An ambitious urban renewal programme has revamped this former port, which has Victoria Harbour at its heart. There are parklands, marinas, apartments, offices, shops, bars, cafés, restaurants and leisure facilities, including the huge Etihad Stadium (Docklands Stadium; www.etihadstadium.com.au). One attraction that has managed to be half Melbourne Eye and half eye sore, is a giant observation wheel, the Melbourne Star (tel: 03-8688 9688; www.melbournestar.com) which was installed in 2008. The 120-metre wheel, with seven spokes to reflect the seven-sided star on the Australian flag, was rebuilt and reopened in December 2013. Also new to Docklands is the O'Brien Group Arena (tel: 1300 756 699; www.obriengrouparena. com.au), an ice-sports and entertainment venue with two Olympic-sized ice rinks, a 1,000-seat stadium and a winter sports gym.

Near the river, just south of the heart of town, on St Kilda Road, an Eiffel Tower–style structure marks the modern **Victorian Arts Centre** (www.artscentremelbourne.com.au). This elegant colour-changing spire rises from flowing curves suggesting a ballet dancer's tutu. The first part of the complex to open, in 1968, was the National Gallery of Victoria, now called **NGV International Ⓐ** (www. ngv.vic.gov.au; daily 10am–5pm; free). The collection showcases international art, old and new. Among the most interesting items on display is a vast Tiepolo painting from the 1740s, *The Banquet of Cleopatra*, plus sculptures by Rodin, Henry Moore and Barbara Hepworth, and a first-class survey of classical Chinese porcelain.

The Ian Potter Centre, at Federation Square, houses the Gallery's wealth of Australian art (see page 167).

The **Theatres Building**, directly beneath the symbolic spire identifying the Arts Centre, is the place for opera, ballet and musicals. Under the same roof are a playhouse for drama and a smaller studio theatre for performances of more intimate works. The adjoining, circular **Hamer Hall**, which seats 2,700 people, is used for symphony concerts, but the acoustics can be changed to suit other types of performance. If you're not going to a concert, nip in for a glance at the artwork in the lobby, or take a guided backstage tour. The complex provides dining opportunities from snack bars to luxury-class restaurants. The Centre also includes a Museum of Performing Arts.

Just across Princes Bridge on the north side of the river, the spires of **St Paul's Cathedral** are not as old as they look; they were added in the 1920s, several decades after the original Gothic-style structure was completed. The church is a refreshing hideaway in the midst of the busiest part of the city, a few steps away from the main suburban railway station, Flinders Street. Also here is a less obvious historic landmark, **Young and Jackson's** (www.youngandjacksons.com.au), whose upstairs bar contains a notorious oil painting of the nude 'Chloe', which has delighted many generations of beer drinkers since it scandalised Melbourne's art exhibition of 1880.

Dame Edna mosaic adorning the Docklands

Just south of St Paul's Cathedral is **Federation Square ®** (www. fedsquare.com; free), a futuristic-looking group of modern buildings built around a public square, which hosts various events, festivals and big-screen broadcasts of major occasions (including World Cup football matches). It also houses the **Ian Potter Centre: NGV Australia** (www.ngv.vic. gov.au; daily 10am–5pm; free), a three-floor space with 20 galleries dedicated to Australian art – contemporary, colonial and indigenous.

From here, stroll through Birrarung Marr, an 8-hectare (20-acre) riverside park that honours the traditional owners, the Wurundjeri people. The name means 'river of mists' in their Woiwurrung language. There are several stunning sculptures and installations, and it's the scene for a number of festivals and events. It's a great spot to watch the Moomba festival, Australia's largest free community event, held on the Yarra annually during the Labour day long weekend (second Monday in March), featuring a floating parade, stalls, fireworks and river sports. A highlight is the Birdman Rally, where wannabe superheroes jump off a 4-metre platform into the Yarra, wearing homemade 'wings' – the person who 'flies' the furthest wins. Famously, while the name is officially supposed to translate into 'let's get together and have fun' in the local indigenous language, rumour has it that the founders of the festival were tricked by their Aboriginal advisers, and Moomba actually means 'up your bum'.

Melbourne **Town Hall**, on the corner of Swanston and Collins Streets, dates from the 1860s. It's used for concerts and official events, and can hold about 3,000 people. It's the central venue for the annual Melbourne Comedy Festival (www.comedyfestival.com. au), which attracts top-quality international acts each March–April.

Collins Street – combined with Bourke Street, which runs parallel, and Bourke Street's various arcades and laneways – are one reason Melburnians claim the best shopping in Australia (other places that add to this reputation are the more boutique-based shopping suburbs of South Yarra and Prahran, and the large factory outlets

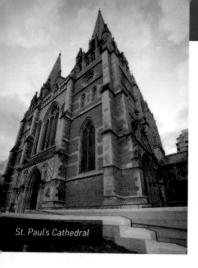
St. Paul's Cathedral

in Richmond and elsewhere). Two large department stores – Myer and David Jones – are located close together in pedestrians-only **Bourke Street Mall**, between Elizabeth and Swanston streets. The outstanding example of an old-time Melbourne shopping institution, the glass-roofed **Block Arcade** (www.the blockarcade.com.au) is an 1892 copy of Milan's Vittorio Emmanuele Galleria. Have afternoon tea at the historic Hopetoun Tea Rooms (www.hopetountearooms.com.au) inside the arcade. The nearby Royal Arcade (www.royalarcade.com.au) is also worth investigating. Also running off Bourke Street Mall are narrow laneways lined with avant-garde boutiques and numerous cafés, which contribute to the city's well-developed coffee culture – considered to be one of the best in the world. Try Cathedral Arcade or Flinders Way for the best of independent and local fashion designers. One end of the mall is dominated by the Victorian-era Melbourne GPO (www.melbournesgpo.com), which has been renovated as a hub for sophisticated fashion and food shopping.

By way of historic buildings, Melbourne likes to show off. The **Parliament of Victoria ⊙**, set in its own park facing Spring Street, has been called the finest legislative headquarters this side of London; many of the furnishings found here are copies of those in Westminster. The federal government used this as its temporary headquarters in the early 20th century, just after Federation. The building is open for guided tours when the state parliament is not sitting.

Older than any of the city's well-preserved Victorian buildings is **Cook's Cottage** in Fitzroy Gardens. The great discoverer never lived in Melbourne; the stone house was transplanted in 1934 from Great Ayton in Cook's native Yorkshire. In truth, it would be more accurate to call it Cook's parents' cottage, since there is no evidence that the good captain ever lived in it.

In Australia, jails are very popular tourist attractions (perhaps not so surprising, given its history). One of the most fascinating is the **Old Melbourne Gaol** (www.oldmelbournegaol.com.au; daily 9.30am–5pm; charge), situated across the road from the modern Police Headquarters on Russell Street. Opened in 1854, the penitentiary was the scene of more than 100 hangings. The death masks of the most famous prisoners are displayed, along with other penal memorabilia, such as a 'lashing triangle', last used in 1958. The best-known character on death row, the celebrated bushranger Ned Kelly, was executed here on Melbourne Cup Day 1880. You can step inside the executive-sized cell that was his last residence on earth; it has a fine view of the gallows. The nearby State Library displays the homemade suit of armour he was wearing when captured.

Within walking distance is the **Royal Exhibition Building**, a beautiful leftover from the 1880 Melbourne International Exhibition. Next to it is a much more modern building housing the **Melbourne Museum** (www.museumvictoria.com.au; daily 10am–5pm; charge), devoted to history, natural history and ethnography. Exhibits include an impressive indoor rainforest, dinosaur skeletons, an Aboriginal culture gallery and a gallery of boats of the Pacific islands.

Melbourne's **Chinatown** centres on Little Bourke Street. Special streetlights and gates define the area, where you'll find Chinese restaurants, cafés, a church and exotic shops. The **Chinese Museum** (www.chinesemuseum.com.au; daily 10am–5pm; charge) documents Chinese immigration history. The area has had

a unique flavour since the gold rush days, when fortune-hunte
from China crowded into this low-rent district before and aft
their efforts out in the bush. Chinatown today glows on the ma
of local gourmets.

As does **Queen Victoria Market** ❺ (www.qvm.com.au), wh
sums up the bounty of Australian agriculture. Just about everythi
that grows can be found here, piled up in irresistibly fresh pyrami
as if the best fruit and vegetables had been borrowed from eve
market from Sweden to Sicily. The best time to take in the atmc
phere (and get the freshest produce) is early morning, but note th
the market is closed on Mondays and Wednesdays. In addition
produce, you will find a flea market.

Parks and gardens

South of the river are the **Royal Botanic Gardens** ❻ (www.rb
vic.gov.au; 7.30am–dusk), classed among the finest in the wor

Queen Victoria Market

Thirty-six hectares (90 acres) of superb rolling landscape remind the visitor that Melbourne has four seasons (often in one day). Each time of year has its specialities, and seasonal leaflets are available for self-guided walks. Over 13,000 species are represented, amid lovely lakes and lawns, including a selection of brightly tinted trees and plants from the Northern Hemisphere. Seasonal open-air film screenings take place here at the Moonlight Cinema (www.moonlight.com.au/melbourne).

Between the Botanic Gardens and Kings Domain is **Government House**, the state governor's mansion, and **La Trobe's Cottage**, its early 19th-century predecessor. The timber cottage was shipped over from Britain to serve as a home for Charles La Trobe, who became Victoria's first Lieutenant-Governor back in 1851. One of La Trobe's achievements was to establish a wine industry in Victoria.

Across from the cottage, the **Shrine of Remembrance** (daily 10am–5pm) was originally built in remembrance of the dead of World War I, but now commemorates those Australians who have fallen in all armed conflicts. Once a year, every Armistice Day at 11am, a beam of sunlight coming through an opening in the roof strikes the Rock of Remembrance. It's a powerful and poignant experience.

The nearby Melbourne Observatory (open for tours only, see www.rbg.vic.gov.au) once housed the largest telescope in the world, the Great Melbourne Telescope.

In Parkville, to the north of the centre, the **Royal Melbourne Zoological Gardens** (www.zoo.org.au; daily 9am–5pm; charge) have kangaroos, koalas and platypuses, plus elephants, giraffes, monkeys and other creatures. In summer, there's evening musical entertainment.

Melbourne's suburbs

The inner-city suburb of **Carlton** – a short tram trip from the city – combines the restored elegance of Victorian architecture with contemporary dynamism. The latter may be attributed to the area's immigrant colony, mostly Italian. Hence there is a great profusion of outdoor cafés, pizzerias, trattorias, pasticcerias and gelaterias.

Lygon Street, Carlton, is Melbourne's very own slice of Italy, replete with numerous pasta restaurants interspersed with wine bars, cheese shops, quality fashion boutiques and delicatessens. Jimmy Watson's (www.jimmywatsons.com) bar and restaurant in Lygon Street is a Melbourne institution.

In **South Yarra**, 2 hectares (5 acres) of lawns and gardens surround Melbourne's finest stately home, **Como House** (www.como house.com.au; daily 10am–5pm; charge) in South Yarra. Now run by the National Trust, this example of the colonial era's high style was completed with the addition of a gold-and-white ballroom in the 1870s.

Toorak, the snootiest of suburbs, is rumoured to harbour more money than any other neighbourhood in Australia. The mansions make tourists and most other passers-by stand and gape. Shops on Toorak Road are full of stylish delights.

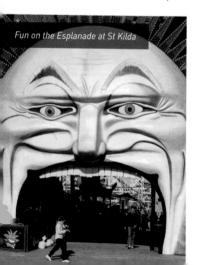

Fun on the Esplanade at St Kilda

A totally different shopping experience awaits in the seaside suburb of **St Kilda**. On Sundays its Esplanade is taken over by artists, antiques dealers and flea market entrepreneurs of every sort. Acland Street's restaurants, cafés and bakeries preserve a middle-European Jewish flavour.

Brunswick Street, in **Fitzroy**, reflects the city's bohemian side. Restaurants and cafés, Spanish bars on nearby Johnston Street, comedy and live-band venues – all buzzing with activity day and night. Fitzroy's streets are crammed with alternative lifestyle shops, second-hand clothing and funky furniture.

EXCURSIONS

A favourite day trip goes out to the **Dandenong Ranges**, volcanic mountains where flowered hillsides and eucalyptus forests make for total relaxation. Only an hour's drive from town, the mountains won't exactly take your breath away; Mt Dandenong itself claims an altitude of only 633 metres (2,077ft).

One highlight of a day among the small towns, farms, parks and gardens is a ride on **Puffing Billy** (www.puffing billy.com.au), a restored steam train plying 13km (8 miles) of narrow-gauge track from Belgrave to Menzies Creek. The line was given over to passenger operations from 1900 to 1958. Four years later it was converted to the tourism business. The train never achieves great speed. In fact, an annual race pits Puffing Billy against hundreds of runners.

The **William Ricketts Sanctuary** (Mt Dandenong Tourist Rd; tel: 03-9751 1300; daily 10am–4.30pm; charge) is an extraordinary collection of sculpture produced by a Caucasian loner who became obsessed with Aboriginal culture and its near-destruction by his fellow whites. Ricketts carved incredibly lifelike faces of Aboriginal people, accompanied by their spiritual symbols. The result of his artistic toils is unorthodox.

In **Sherbrooke Forest Park**, part of Dandenong Ranges National Park, you can give your lungs a treat, savouring the elixir of ferns and mountain ash and whatever flowers happen to be in bloom. The forest is immensely tall, with mountain ash monuments as high as 20-storey buildings and ferns as big as palm trees. This is the place to see – or at least hear – the lyrebird, a great mimic; it does imitations of other birds, human voices and even of inanimate objects such as passing cars. Among the residents of the park are the echidna (a hedgehog-like anteater), the platypus and the koala.

Healesville, less than 60km (37 miles) to the east of Melbourne, is the place to go for an intimate look at Australian animals on their home ground. **Healesville Sanctuary** (www.zoo.org.au/healesville sanctuary; daily 9am–5pm; charge), nearby in the **Yarra Valley**, contains more than 200 native species such as kangaroos, wombats and emus. The sanctuary was founded in 1921 as a research establishment for the study of local fauna, and is committed to the care and conservation of Australian wildlife.

The Yarra Valley was the site of the first commercial winery in the state, dating back to the middle of the 19th century. The region's vineyards, numbering about 80, are world-class; well worth a wine-tasting outing or a visit to one of the winery restaurants.

Another wine region near Melbourne is the **Mornington Peninsula**, an 80-minute drive south of the city. In addition to the

Yarra Valley

50 wineries with cellar doors, there are beaches (bay and ocean-facing), national parks, coastal walking trails, lovely rural scenery and pleasant villages such as Red Hill, Shoreham and Flinders.

PHILLIP ISLAND

For a magical experience for both adults and children, try a long day-trip to **Phillip Island** ㉚ (www.visitphillipisland.com), 120km (75 miles) southeast of Melbourne, home of the fairy penguins (also known as little penguins), the world's smallest members of the penguin family. Hundreds of these engaging birds, standing only about 40cm (16in) high and looking quite formal in their blue-grey plumage with white fronts, come home to their burrows at sunset. The number varies depending on activities at sea, where they spend most of their time fishing. For reasons of their own, perhaps sensing danger, they tread water offshore until night falls, and only then do they venture onto the beach. After decades of being stared at, they still feel insecure arriving on the island.

Before dusk falls, hundreds of tourists gather behind ropes on Summerland Beach and in viewing platforms on the sandhills above for the Penguin Parade (www.penguins.org.au; charge). You're not allowed to upset the penguins: no flash photography, no running, no sudden movement. The penguins observe all this and wait for the first star to appear in the sky. Then the first brave penguin scout scrambles onto dry land and cautiously lurches across the beach and up the hill to its burrow. In small groups the others follow, waddling through the sand dunes up to their burrows right at sunset, just as their ancestors have done night after night for thousands of generations. It can take an hour or more for all the birds to get ashore – take warm clothes, for the nights are chilly even in summer.

Nearby you'll find signs to The Nobbies and Seal Rocks, home to the country's largest Australian fur seal colony (early December, the peak of the breeding season, is the best time to see them) – and plenty of great white sharks too, who come to feed on them, although this doesn't seem to worry the surfers at the neighbouring beach.

Other attractions include a historic heritage farm (on Churchill Island, accessed from Phillip Island) and a Koala Conservation Centre.

WILSONS PROMONTORY

Until the Ice Age, the southernmost tip of the Australian mainland was connected to Tasmania. When the ice melted the heights

Kangaroos in 'The Prom'

became an island. Since then the dunes have built up, linking the massive promontory to the rest of Victoria. The varied and spectacular scenery has made **Wilsons Promontory** ③ the state's most popular national park (so popular that camping spots are assigned via a lottery at peak times), which is making a recovery from some devastating bush fires in 2009.

The coastline ranges from magnificent granite headlands to peaceful sandy beaches. Walking trails wander through forests and moorland and flower-covered heathland. Wombats, koalas, kangaroos, wallabies and emus can all be seen here. Known locally as 'The Prom', the peninsula is about 240km (150 miles) southeast of Melbourne.

THE GOLDFIELDS

A drive of 113km (70 miles) west of Melbourne takes you well over a century back in time to the town of **Ballarat** ②, rich with all the atmosphere of Australia's golden age. This is real gold-rush country, and it is still a prize destination for tourists.

Ballarat has a bittersweet history. Gold was discovered in 1851, and thousands of miners trekked to the fields. The early arrivals simply scooped up a fortune, but latecomers had to work harder, following the ore ever deeper.

Almost from the outset the government collected a licence fee from the miners. Many newcomers couldn't afford to pay a tax, so they tended to lie low when the licence inspectors swooped. In the midst of growing antagonism between the authorities and the miners, charges of murder and official corruption pushed the diggers to revolt. In the Eureka Rebellion, insurgent miners were besieged in their stockade. A battle cost 35 people their lives, mostly diggers. The anguish endured for years, inspiring poets and politicians.

When peace returned to the goldfields, and many of the miners' grievances were answered, Ballarat went back to the business of making a fortune. In 1858 a group of Cornishmen came upon what

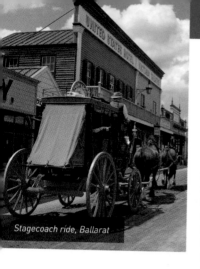
Stagecoach ride, Ballarat

they called the Welcome Nugget, weighing in at an enormous 63,000g (2,220oz). It was eventually put on show in the Crystal Palace in London before being minted.

To see what Ballarat was like in the 1850s, visit **Sovereign Hill** (www.sovereign hill.com.au; daily 10am–5pm; charge), an open-air museum recreating the sights, sounds and smells of the gold rush. Local people dressed in Victorian-era clothing operate the old shops, post office, bakery and printing office of what appears to be a real town. Tourists are invited to try their hand with a digger's pan. The **Gold Museum** (daily 9.30am–5.30pm; charge) traces the history of the mineral since biblical times and displays nuggets and gold coins. The Eureka Rebellion is re-created nightly in the show 'Blood on the Southern Cross'.

In the real Ballarat, the principal public buildings on the town's wide tree-lined streets are a long-lasting monument to the good old days. Some of those who got rich quick had the good taste to spend some of their money on the finer things, hence the statues of mythological subjects in marble in the **Botanical Gardens**, and the admirable collection of early Australian art housed in the **Art Gallery of Ballarat** (daily 10am–5pm; charge).

Another treat for nostalgia fans is the town of **Bendigo**, situated 150km (93 miles) northwest of Melbourne. The town's unusual name is a very roundabout corruption of Abednego, the Old Testament companion of Shadrach and Meshach. In the 1850s,

Bendigo Creek, running through the centre of town, was besieged with panning miners.

The **Central Deborah Mine** (www.central-deborah.com; daily 9.30am–4.30pm; charge), the last commercial mine to operate in Bendigo, is now a museum; a visit includes a one-hour underground mine tour. From the mine you can take a 'Talking Tram', an antique vehicle rigged up for tourists on an 8km (5 mile) itinerary. The last stop is the **joss house** (Chinese temple). One curiosity of Bendigo was the size of the Chinese population. Chinese miners worshipped in a prayer house constructed of timber and handmade bricks. The remains that stand today are filled with relics of the early Chinese fortune hunters.

THE GREAT OCEAN ROAD

Beyond **Torquay** is the beginning of the **Great Ocean Road** ㊳, which skirts nearly 200km (125 miles) of spectacular coastline and is

View from the Great Ocean Road

undoubtedly one of the world's most beautiful drives. It was built by ex-servicemen of World War I in homage to their comrades killed at the front.

A great number of ships have gone aground in these treacherous waters. Along **Shipwreck Coast**, the wrecks of more than 80 sailing vessels rest on the seabed. Rising above the road are the bush-covered Otway Ranges, most of which fall within **Great Otway National Park**, which has many bushwalking options. The surf provides recreation, too. **Bells Beach**, situated between Torquay and Anglesea, hosts the Bells Surfing Classic every Easter. Just before you reach Lorne, follow the signs for **Erskine Falls**, splendid cascades that are worth the 20-minute detour. **Lorne** and, further west, **Apollo Bay** are popular seaside resorts, well provided with restaurants, cafés and shops. From Apollo Bay, the Great Ocean Road leaves the coast to wind through the forest behind **Cape Otway**, where the lighthouse has watched over the entrance to the Bass Strait since 1848.

Twelve Apostles

Beyond Princetown lies the spectacular coastline of **Port Campbell National Park**, where breakers have battered the soft limestone cliffs, creating grottoes and gorges, arches and sea-sculptures rising from the surf. The Great Ocean Road allows occasional glimpses of the drama below, which includes the stark rock stacks known as the **Twelve Apostles** and the spray billowing through **London Arch**. Take time to stop at all the vantage points.

After Peterborough and the spectacular Bay of Islands comes **Warrnambool** (www.visitwarrnambool.com.au), once a busy port and now a pastoral and holiday centre. Warrnambool has become known as the 'southern right whale nursery', with these magnificent animals visiting the waters here to give birth between late May and early October. Whales and their newborn calves can often be seen (and heard) from Logan's Beach. Around the original lighthouse is the **Flagstaff Hill Maritime Museum** (www.flagstaffhill.com; daily 9am–5pm; charge), a re-creation of a 19th-century port, complete with shipwrights, chandlers and sailmakers.

Along the coast is the fishing-village charm of **Port Fairy**, where brightly painted boats tie up at the jetty with their catches of lobster and crab. Port Fairy Bay was named by Captain James Wishart who brought his tiny cutter, the *Fairy*, into the Moyne River to find shelter during a sealing expedition in 1810, but the town was called Belfast for a period. Sealers and, later, whalers built quaint stone cottages which still nestle under the tall Norfolk Island pines shading the streets. In March each year, a very popular three-day folk festival draws music lovers to the town.

TASMANIA

If you think of Tasmania as the last stop before the South Pole, you're right: Antarctic expeditions actually set sail from Hobart. No matter what direction you're heading in, it's a staging post you will hate to leave. Tasmania's scenery owes more to solar than polar

Hobart and Mount Wellington at dawn

influences. Although snow covers the hills in winter, it's a verdant island enjoying a temperate climate.

Suspended 240km (149 miles) to the south of southernmost mainland Australia, Tasmania is small only by the swollen standards of the continent. With an area of approximately 68,000 sq km (26,250 sq miles), it's bigger than Sri Lanka and Switzerland.

'Tassie', as the state is familiarly known, calls itself the Holiday Isle and pushes tourism. Its early residents would have had a bitter laugh at that, interspersed with an oath or two, for the island used to be the place where incorrigible prisoners were sent. While humble embezzlers and petty larcenists were transported to Sydney, the batterers and escape artists tended to be tagged for Tasmania.

Early explorers happened upon Tasmania because it lies on the 40th parallel – the Roaring Forties – along which an unfailing westerly wind blows around the globe. Their sailing ships could hardly miss the place. But that's not to diminish the achievement of the Dutch navigator Abel Tasman, who discovered the island in 1642. He named it after his sponsor, Anton van Diemen, governor of the Dutch East Indies.

The Dutch never saw a future for Van Diemen's Land, and Britain eventually claimed the island simply to cut out the French. Because of the cruel conditions inflicted on the prisoners, Van Diemen's Land acquired a sinister reputation. The very mention of the name could send a shiver down a sinner's spine. The transportation of convicts was abolished in 1852, and three years later the name was changed to Tasmania in memory of its discoverer and to improve the state's image.

Since then, Tasmania has become something of a tourist paradise. One day, some brilliant entrepreneur may put it on the world map and the crowds will arrive. Until then, if you like wild scenery, open moors, green hills, deserted beaches, Georgian architecture, temperate-climate forests, uncrowded towns and open-hearted people, you could become a Tasmaniac.

⊙ WIPING OUT THE ABORIGINES

When Van Diemen's Land was first settled, the island's Aboriginal people are estimated to have numbered between 3,000 and 7,000. They were different from the indigenous mainland peoples, in looks and culture. As the British seized the land and wiped out the animals and birds that the indigenous tribes needed for food, the Aborigines fought back with punitive attacks. Enraged, the white men retaliated with all the force at their disposal. The survivors of this genocide were exiled to Flinders Island in the Bass Strait, an outpost best known for its shipwrecks. Although there were belated efforts to protect the people, the last of the full-blooded Tasmanian tribespeople died in 1876. They were not entirely exterminated, however, as mixed-blood descendants of the Aboriginal women who had been abducted by British and American whalers and sealers and taken to islands in the Bass Strait (including Flinders) founded a flourishing Aboriginal movement.

Boats moored in Hobart Harbour

HOBART

Everybody knows that Sydney Harbour is the exciting one, glamorous and instantly recognisable the world over. **Hobart** ③④ is the lovable harbour, a perfect ocean port on the Derwent River, with soft mountains rising beyond. It might have been transplanted from quite another seafaring latitude, as brisk and tidy as Bergen or Helsinki.

You never know what kind of ships you'll see here: freighters, fishing boats, luxury yachts or ice breakers. Sail power still matters here: Hobart's Constitution Dock is the finishing line of the gruelling Sydney to Hobart yacht race.

Hobart, Australia's second oldest capital city, has kept a powerful array of historic monuments, from stately official buildings to quaint cottages. Best of all, they're still in use.

With a population of around 225,000 (suburbs included), Hobart is small enough to get around and get to know, and as unsophisticated and satisfying as the local fish and chips.

In this deepwater port, the ships come right into the centre of town, to **Sullivans Cove**. The waterfront, always colourful, is the place to begin exploring the city on foot or by taking a cruise from Brooke Street. You can watch crates of giant crabs, lobsters and scallops coming ashore, and follow their destiny to the floating fast-food restaurants moored at **Constitution Dock**, where the yacht races end. There's a choice of waterfront bars, cafés and restaurants, mostly fish-themed, alongside and at trendy Elizabeth Street pier and Murray Street pier.

Also bordering the docks, **Salamanca Place** (www.salamanca. com.au) is home to a long row of sandstone warehouses from the 1830s, now occupied by artisans' workshops, boutiques and restaurants. On Saturday, the huge **Salamanca Market** (8.30am–3pm) takes over, with stalls selling various arts and crafts, knick-knacks, flowers and vegetables, while buskers perform and pass the hat. Behind Salamanca Place, Salamanca Square is fringed with lively al fresco cafés, restaurants and bars.

Altogether more serious is **Parliament House**, built in 1840, also facing the waterfront. The state's bicameral legislature operates in a low-rise stone building, which displays some admirable architectural details. Another venerable structure still in use is the **Theatre Royal** on Campbell Street, Australia's oldest live theatre. Built in a luxurious style in 1834, it has featured stars like Noel Coward and Laurence Olivier.

Overlooking Salamanca Place, and reached on foot by Kelly's Steps, **Battery Point** is the historic heart of Hobart. The battery in question was a set of coastal artillery guns installed in 1818. Ten years later signal flags were added, for relaying the big news of the day, such as ship arrivals or prison escapes. The area is worth an hour or two of exploration to absorb the atmosphere of the narrow streets, the mansions and cottages, churches and taverns. National Trust volunteers lead excellent walking tours (tel: 03-6344 6233 for bookings). One of the colonial mansions is now the **Narryna Heritage Museum** (www.narr yna.com.au; Tue-Sat 10am–4.30pm, Sun 12pm–4.30pm; charge), with period furnishings, vintage vehicles and various farm implements.

The **Tasmanian Museum and Art Gallery** (www.tmag.tas.gov.au; daily 10am–4pm; free) is worth visiting for the collection relating to the Tasmanian tiger (thylacine). This striped, dog-like marsupial is believed to have been hunted to extinction by the 1930s, but some people swear they have seen living ones. If you prefer marine exhibits, visit the **Maritime Museum of Tasmania** (www.maritimetas.org; daily 9am–5pm; charge), in Argyle Street.

The centre of Hobart is linked to the suburbs and the airport by the graceful **Tasman Bridge** across the Derwent River.

For a panorama of Hobart and the valley of the Derwent River, ascend **Mt Wellington**. You can forget your mountain-climbing equipment. A paved road goes all the way to the summit, 1,270m (4,167ft) above the sea, but there's also a rugged footpath. It often snows on the mountain in the winter months, but it rarely blocks the road.

EXCURSIONS FROM HOBART

A popular tourist destination up the river at Claremont used to be the **Cadbury chocolate factory** . Fans of Willy Wonka just loved it. The factory still manufactures chocolate here but, unfortunately, the visitor centre is no longer in operation.

Those with a more savoury tooth might prefer touring the imposing **Cascade Brewery** (www.cascadebreweryco.com.au; daily guided tours), the oldest in Australia, at 140 Cascade Road. The excellent beers, made with pure Tasmanian water, are famously labelled with a Tasmanian tiger logo.

At the Moorilla winery on the Berriedale peninsula in Hobart, Mona (Museum of Old and New Art, www.mona.net.au; Wed–Mon 10am–5pm, until 6pm in summer; charge for non-Tasmanians) is one of Australia's most interesting art galleries – but be warned, many of its exhibits are not for the prudish.

At **Taroona**, situated beyond Wrest Point Casino at upmarket Sandy Bay, you can visit the remains of a different kind of factory, the **Shot Tower**. Though it looks like an ordinary chimney, this

48-metre (157-ft) high tower, built in 1870, was used in the manufacture of gunshot and musket balls. You can climb the internal spiral staircase (300 or so steps) to the very summit for a view of the countryside and the Derwent Estuary.

A complex of modern office buildings at **Kingston** is the working headquarters for Australia's extensive operations in the neighbourhood of the South Pole. The Commonwealth Antarctic Division coordinates logistics and research in fields such as glaciology, botany, physics and medicine.

PORT ARTHUR

Tasmania's most-visited historic highlight is the penal colony of **Port Arthur** ③⑤ (www.portarthur.org.au; daily 9am–dusk; charge), an hour's drive from Hobart on the scenic Tasman Peninsula. Be sure to visit some of the spectacular natural features such as the Blowhole, Pirates Bay Lookout and Tasman Arch on the way there. Port Arthur's past is so grim, you'll be astonished at just how picturesque it looks. Founded in 1830 as Australia's ultimate prison settlement, Port Arthur supposedly housed the most intractable convicts – those who had committed second offences after being transported to Australia – plus a few political prisoners, including some Irish rebels. It rapidly became one of the world's most-dreaded institutions.

Chain gangs, toiling under the lash, built these stone

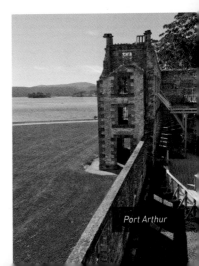

Port Arthur

buildings, which have survived for more than a century. The story is detailed at the visitor centre, as well as in the compelling **museum** in what used to be the penal colony's asylum.

The biggest building still standing, at four storeys high, was designed originally as a storehouse but became a penitentiary for 650 inmates. Other surviving buildings are the **Asylum** (many prisoners went mad) and, next door, the '**Model Prison**'. Both have been restored. Convicts designed and built a large church, now in picturesque ruins. Its 13 spires represent Christ and the apostles. Then there is the mortuary, which did a lively business; more than 1,700 graves occupy the nearby **Isle of the Dead**. Other than by dying, Port Arthur was practically escape-proof, with sharks waiting on one side of the narrow Eaglehawk Neck and half-starved killer dogs on the other. In total, some 10,000 prisoners did time at Port Arthur during its 47 years of operation.

Port Arthur's tragic history was added to in 1996, when it was the scene of Australia's worst mass murder – an indiscriminate attack by a lone gunman, which left 35 people dead, including several members of the facility's staff. A tasteful memorial can be seen in the grounds, but it's tactful not to ask too many questions – many of the guides and workers were there on the day and memories remain raw.

Admission to Port Arthur includes a brief walking tour and a harbour cruise, leaving from the information centre. Boats run twice daily

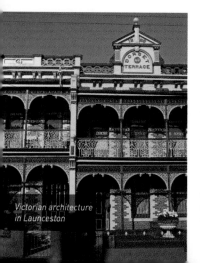

Victorian architecture in Launceston

to the Isle of the Dead. Avid ghost hunters should take the famous Port Arthur Ghost Tour run nightly – bookings are essential.

> **Wine appreciation**
>
> The wineries around Launceston offer tastings, and most of them also have very good restaurants.

LAUNCESTON

Tasmania's second city is an agreeable, roomy town at the head of the Tamar River. Launceston exudes an English flavour, with elm trees, rosebushes, and patriotic statues and plaques. The journey north from Hobart skirts soft green hills studded with sheep. In the villages, to enliven the scene, the houses have roofs the colour of fire engines.

Launceston was founded in the year 1805, as Patersonia. Soon afterwards, the name was changed to match that of the town of Launceston in Cornwall, the birthplace of the colony's governor. The historic aspects of the town are well preserved, starting in the centre, the **Civic Square**, the location of the **Macquarie House** (1830). Restored to mint condition, this historic building is now a café.

The main building of the **Queen Victoria Museum** (daily 10am–4pm; free), situated just a short stroll away on Wellington Street, has something for everyone, from stuffed platypuses to blunderbusses and prisoners' chains. One surprising attraction here is an intact Chinese temple (joss house), which originally served the Chinese tin miners in the Tasmanian town of Weldborough. Downstairs, the Queen Vic Café is one of Launceston's best. The museum's art collection has moved to the striking new Inveresk site, a multi-million-dollar transformation of a railway yard on the North Esk River.

Tasmania is known for its talented craftspeople, whose output is on show at the **Design Centre** (www.designcentre.com.au; Mon–Fri 9.30am–5.30pm, Sat–Sun 10am–4pm; charge), on the western edge of City Park. The highlight is the collection of contemporary furniture made from various species of Tasmanian timber.

Cataract Gorge, a stirring geological feature, is within walking distance of the centre of town. Here the South Esk River slices between steep cliffs on its way to the Tamar. There are hiking trails, boating opportunities and, for sightseers who don't suffer queasy spells, a chairlift – the longest single-span lift in the world at 308 metres (336yds) – spans the canyon. Nearby is the **James Boag Brewery Experience** (www.boags.com.au; Mon–Fri 9.30am–5pm, Sat-Sun 10.30am–4pm; free), housed in the historic Tamar Hotel, where you can take a tour of the brewery that makes one of Australia's best beers (tel: 03-6332 6300 for tour bookings).

WILDERNESS

Much of the southwestern quarter of Tasmania is untouched by civilisation. There is a reason why it has remained unspoilt: it's often unapproachable by road. Four-wheel-drive vehicles, canoes, rafts or just sturdy legs are the best methods of penetrating these wild places. In Tasmania a higher percentage of the total land area has been made national park than in any other state.

Even so, attempts by various commercial interests to log or dam unspoiled wilderness regions have triggered clashes with Tasmania's strong conservationist movement. The Wilderness Society (www.wilderness.org.au) campaigns to save the state's remaining stands of old-growth forest available for logging.

The best known Wilderness Society campaign was the successful Franklin Blockade of 1982, which helped save the wild Franklin River from damming. Base for the campaigners was the West Coast fishing port of Strahan, which now derives its income from scenic cruises on the pristine Gordon River (into which the Franklin flows) and flights over the Franklin, which can also be experienced on gruelling four- to 10-day rafting trips. The West Coast Wilderness Railway (tel: 03-6471 0100 for bookings; www.wcwr.com.au), a redevelopment of a 19th-century line, now links Strahan to the nearby town of Queenstown, its surrounding hills once laid bare by the

Cradle Mountain, Tasmania

effects of decades of copper mining and smelting, but now gradually becoming green as plants re-grow.

South West National Park, covering most of the southwestern corner of Tasmania, has a variety of spectacular scenery, including rugged mountains, glacial lakes, icy rivers and forests of giant Antarctic beech trees – a grand adventure playground for experienced, well-prepared hikers.

Much more accessible is **Cradle Mountain–Lake St Clair National Park**, a few hours' drive northwest of Hobart. Here you'll find a wonderland carved out by glaciers: craggy mountain peaks, lakes and tarns, alpine heathlands and extensive buttongrass plains. Extending through the length of the park, from the jagged grandeur of Cradle Mountain reflected in tranquil Dove Lake, south to the glacier-gouged deepwater basin of Lake St Clair, is the 80km (50-mile) Overland Track, a wilderness walk that takes at least five days to complete. But it's not necessary to exert yourself: you can enjoy day walks and the breath-taking scenery from very comfortable lodges located at Cradle Mountain or Lake St Clair.

North Sydney's Olympic pool with the Harbour Bridge in the background

WHAT TO DO

SPORT

Sport in Australia is inescapable, from the dawn jogger puffing past your window to the football crowds celebrating late into the night with shouting, songs and car horns. In a country so beautiful, and with a climate so benign, you'll be tempted to join the sporting crowds, either playing games yourself or watching the professionals. Under the dependable sun, everything is possible, from skiing – on water or snow – to surfing to sailing.

Spectator sports are also a passion. You can measure their impact by the newspapers, with their comprehensive sports sections, and by the amount of live sports coverage and results on television and radio. If Australians are not playing a game or watching it, they're most likely betting on the result, or at least arguing about it.

In what other country could a racehorse be as revered as is Phar Lap, winner of the 1930 Melbourne Cup? When he died, after a heroic victory in the United States, flags flew at half-mast in Sydney. Today Phar Lap's body is the star attraction in Melbourne Museum, and his mighty heart is preserved at the National Museum of Australia in Canberra. The Melbourne Cup race itself brings the nation to a temporary halt as everyone tunes in to listen.

Sporting tastes have changed over time. More than a century ago, a guidebook gloomily reported that very little hunting was available around Sydney, except when 'occasionally parties are made up for rabbit, wallaby or kangaroo shooting'. In 1903 the first car race was run in Australia. Three years later surf bathing in the daytime became legal in Sydney, and waterskiing caught on in 1936. Australia won the Davis Cup in 1939. When Melbourne hosted the

Olympic Games in 1956, Australian athletes seized 35 of the medals. The world was becoming aware of Australia as one of the foremost sporting powers, a nation of aggressive competitors who could become champions in fields as varied as tennis and swimming, cricket and golf, athletics and rugby.

In 1983, joyous delirium swept the nation when the yacht *Australia II* captured the America's Cup. In 2000, at the Sydney Olympics, Australia came fourth in the medal tally (after the US, Russia and China), and at the 2006 Melbourne Commonwealth Games athletes collected a record number of medals. Australia's achievements in out-performing countries like Germany, France, Britain and Japan is even more remarkable considering its population – just about 24.5 million.

The flipside to such success is that, when it doesn't go to plan, the nation barely seems able to cope. After boxing above their footballing (soccer) weight in the 2006 FIFA World Cup in Germany, the team's early exit in South Africa four years later hit hard, and the lacklustre performance of the swimming team in the 2012 London Olympics led to much collective wringing of hands and airing of dirty Speedos in public, while the overall medal tally from the 2016 Rio Olympics was even lower again.

Watersports

Australia's endless coastline provides enough beaches, coves and ports to keep the nation in the water all year round. If that isn't enough, there are lakes, rivers and swimming pools, both Olympic-size and backyard versions. Watersports of every variety are here for the taking.

Swimming in the Indian Ocean, the Tasman Sea, or the Coral Sea is memory-building material, but the surf can be as dangerous as it is invigorating. Most popular beaches have flags showing where it's safe to swim. Beware of undertows and rip tides, and always obey lifeguard's instructions. Sharks are a (very remote) risk in some areas, with occasional attacks on bathers and surfers. If a shark alert is sounded, get out of the water. Also avoid swimming in murky water, with dogs or close to outflows (river mouths and stormwater pipes).

In spite of their mild-sounding name, box jellyfish are a serious seasonal danger in the tropical north, as are tiny but extremely venomous irukandji; elsewhere there may be Portuguese men-of-war, sea snakes or other silent menaces. Check locally before you get in. Most importantly, before you stretch out on the beach, make sure you protect yourself from the sun, which is more powerful than you think with a high UV factor. Light complexions are particularly vulnerable to quick, painful sunburn and worse.

Snorkelling brings you into intimate contact with a brilliant new world full of multicoloured fish and coral. The sport requires a minimum of equipment – a mask and snorkel and, optionally, flippers. Practically anyone can learn how to snorkel in a matter of minutes. Take your own gear, especially when visiting resorts, where they charge a fortune to rent very basic equipment.

Scuba diving with an air tank is the advanced version of snorkelling. The best place in Australia for scuba outings – arguably the best place in the world – is the coral wonderland of the Great Barrier Reef. Many of the resort islands are equipped for all the needs of divers, though you may wish to bring your own snorkel, mask and fins. Many companies offer scuba instruction starting in the swimming

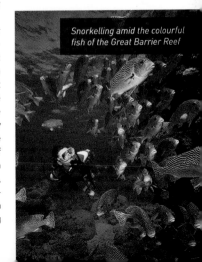

Snorkelling amid the colourful fish of the Great Barrier Reef

pool or a quiet cove, and leading up to an Open Water Certificate. Elsewhere along Australia's coasts, scuba divers devote themselves to exploring submerged wrecks and kelp forests.

Surfing was first documented by Captain Cook, who came across it in Hawaii. He wrote: 'The boldness and address with which we saw them perform these difficult and dangerous manoeuvres was altogether astonishing...' It was nearly two centuries before the first world championships were to be held in Sydney. Two of the best-known beaches to learn the craft are Sydney's Bondi and Manly, but there are many other fine locations up and down the coast of New South Wales. Although Queensland's Surfers Paradise may be just that, many beginners prefer the rollers further north at Noosa. Victoria's most popular surfing area is around Torquay, gateway to the famous waves of Bells Beach. On the west coast, easily accessible world-class surfing beaches close to Perth include those around Bunbury and Margaret River.

Surfing is a popular hobby along Australia's coasts

Boating. Visiting yachts and their crews will always get a warm Aussie-style welcome. At popular resorts, for instance along the Gold Coast or the Great Barrier Reef, yachts and powerboats can be chartered, with or without a professional skipper. Inland, you can command a sailing boat or a houseboat on the relaxing Murray River. Or you might just want to settle for an hour's rental of a pedal boat.

Fishing. In most states you'll need a licence to fish

on inland or coastal waters. Outstanding trout fishing is found in Tasmania, Victoria and the Snowy Mountains. Seasons and bag limits vary from state to state. As for game fishing, the challenge of the giant black marlin is best met off the northern coast of Queensland. If your catch weighs less than half a tonne, it's polite to throw the little fellow back. Or settle for tuna, mackerel or sailfish. Good deep-sea fishing is also found off the coast of Western Australia, especially at Geraldton, and in the Spencer Gulf, near Adelaide. In the tropical northern rivers, a coveted game fish is the barramundi – a great fighter prized for its delicate flesh.

> ### Lifesaving
>
> The world's first surf lifesaving club was set up at Bondi Beach in 1906. The first surfboard riders took to the water in 1915.

Sports ashore

Golf. The landscaping may be foreign, the climate may be a better year-round bet than you're accustomed to, but the game's the same. Melbourne considers itself the nation's golfing capital, with championship courses such as Victoria and the Royal Melbourne. All the cities have golf clubs; they often operate under exchange agreements with clubs overseas, or you may have to be introduced by a local member. With no formality at all you can rent a set of clubs and play at one of the public courses to be found in all the sizeable towns. Golf is also a popular spectator sport in Australia. The Australian Open (www.australianopengolf.com.au) takes place in November.

Tennis. Having produced so many top tennis champions, Australia takes the game seriously. You'll find good courts available in most towns and resorts; some rent rackets and shoes. If you're just watching, then join the crowd. The world's top tennis stars usually tour Australia in December and January. Melbourne Park

'Aussie Rules'

'Aussie Rules' was first played by Victoria gold miners in the 1850s, and the Melbourne Football Club was founded in 1858 – but the game's official rules were not established until 1866.

hosts the Australian Open (www.ausopen.com), one of the tennis world's four Grand Slam tournaments, in January every year.

Bushwalking (hiking). All over Australia there are numerous national parks boasting excellent walking tracks suitable for a wide range of abilities. If you are thinking of doing a long walk, make sure you have a map and compass, good footwear, and adequate clothing and provisions (especially water). Always consult local park offices for advice and up-to-date condition reports (for inclement weather and bush-fire danger especially), and inform someone of your plans and expected return.

Snow sports. The white season in the Australian Alps usually lasts from June to September. The best of the ski resorts in the Snowy Mountains, straddling the border of New South Wales and Victoria, include Thredbo Village, Perisher Valley and Smiggin Holes (NSW) and Mt Buller, Falls Creek, Mt Hotham and Mt Baw Baw (Victoria).

Football and rugby

In Australia the subject of football is so vast and complex – for a start, four different codes are played – that the stranger is likely to be left gasping on the sidelines. But since the country is crazy about it, at least a few definitions may be useful. Incidentally, whatever type of football is being discussed, the fans are likely to call it 'footy'.

Australian Rules Football ('Aussie Rules') was first intro-duced in Melbourne in 1858, and although the Australian Football League (AFL) now includes teams in most major cities, the sport is passionately supported in Victoria, South Australia, Western Australia, the Northern Territory and Tasmania, and finds its most fanatical following in and around Melbourne. It is estimated that every winter Saturday in the city, one person in 16 attends an AFL game, and thousands more follow the saturation TV coverage. The Grand Final, held at the Melbourne Cricket Ground in September, is one of the world's great sporting experiences, rivalling an English FA Cup Final or an American Super Bowl for colour, passion and atmosphere.

The sport, played by 18-aside teams on a cricket oval and combining elements of rugby, Gaelic football and soccer, is characterised by athleticism and bravery. Matches are divided into 25-minute quarters, but the clock stops when the ball isn't in play, and games can last hours.

Rugby League started as a 13-man alternative to Rugby Union, and is played today nationally through the National Rugby League (NRL) competition, although the sport's heartlands are Sydney, Brisbane and Canberra. It's a roughhouse game, physical rather than cerebral, based on an uncompromising masochistic style of defence that prompted one American football coach to observe: 'Our guys could never stand up to that sort of constant punishment.' League attendances are nothing like as large as those of the AFL, but the Sydney clubs – such as St George Illawarra Dragons, Penrith Panthers, Manly Sea Eagles

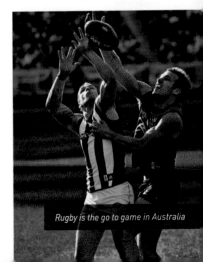

Rugby is the go to game in Australia

and Parramatta Eels – keep their star players fabulously well paid through TV rights deals and revenue from their licensed clubs. The national side, the Kangaroos, regularly hop through tours of France and Great Britain unbeaten.

Rugby Union, the 15-aside, formerly amateur version of the game, is fast, rough and engrossing to the fans. Compared with Rugby League, the game traditionally had a 'silvertail' (upper-crust) image based partly on its strength in the universities and private schools. Now that Union is fully professional, the gentlemanly spirit is less in evidence, but the pro game is far more skilful and fluid. Since 1995, teams representing Queensland, New South Wales and the Australian Capital Territory have competed every winter in the Super 12 tournament, against sides from New Zealand and South Africa. The Australian national team, the Wallabies, regularly competes in the Six Nations and Tri-Nations, as well as the World Cup, which it has won twice.

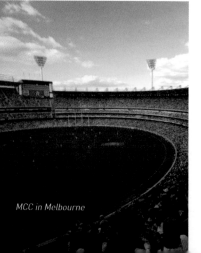

MCC in Melbourne

Soccer is the oldest of the country's football games but, compared with the three other species, is the poor relation. It kicked off in the 19th century among earnest British migrants, more or less stagnated until after World War II, then was revitalised by the arrival of immigrants from southern Europe. Today most clubs in the A-League are dominated by players from the Italian, Greek, Croatian, Serbian, Maltese, Dutch and Macedonian communities.

The Australian national team is called the Socceroos; after a brief appearance in West Germany in 1974, they had a long absence from the world stage before qualifying for the last three World Cups (2006, 2010 and 2014).

Other spectator sports

Cricket has been played in Australia since the early days of the penal colony. The climate is perfect for the traditional five-day test format, and the Ashes contest against the old foe, England, is one of the most hotly fought rivalries in world sport and a fantastic spectacle (especially the Boxing Day test in Melbourne's MCG). It's loaded with symbolism ever since a satirical obituary published in a British newspaper after Australia beat England at The Oval in 1882, stated that English cricket had died, and 'the body will be cremated and the ashes taken to Australia'. Throughout the 90s and early 2000s the Australian team boasted such a wealth of talent that English cricket was repeatedly put to death, but the retirement of several key players saw them lose their mojo and three consecutive Ashes series between 2009–13. During the 2013–14 series, they trounced a fragile England side, but the following series belonged once again to England.

The cricket season extends from October to the end of March, with matches played at interstate level (the Sheffield Shield), down through district ranks to the junior and social levels. The one-day game is popular too.

Horseracing. Practically every Australian town has a racecourse, and betting on horses (or anything else), is as Australian as ice-cold

Birdsville Races

Every September in the remote Queensland Outback town of Birdsville, the Birdsville Picnic Races (www.birdsvilleraces.com) attract enormous crowds. The population of Birdsville leaps from 30 to 3,000 overnight, with many spectators arriving by light planes from all over Australia.

beer. The biggest race of the turf season is the Melbourne Cup, a two-mile classic that is followed so obsessively that the day it's run – the first Tuesday in November – is a public holiday in Victoria. Even the process of government is suspended so that the nation's decision-makers in Canberra can watch the live telecast. **Trotting** (harness racing) and **greyhound racing** are also popular betting-based spectacles that draw crowds of punters.

Motor racing. The biggest race on the calendar is the Australian Formula 1 Grand Prix at Albert Park in Melbourne, but fans of

✪ AUSTRALIAN CHAMPIONS

Australia has bred many world-class winners. Below are some of the pre-eminent sporting personalities of the 20th and 21st centuries:

Athletics
Herb Elliott, Ron Clarke, Robert DeCastella, Sally Pearson

Motor racing
Jack Brabham, Alan Jones, Mark Webber

Cricket
Don Bradman, Greg Chappell, Dennis Lillee, Ricky Ponting, Shane Warne

Golf
Peter Thompson, Greg Norman, Stuart Appleby, Ian Baker-Finch, Wayne Grady, Adam Scott

Swimming
Dawn Fraser, Samantha Riley, Kieren Perkins, Grant Hackett, Ian Thorpe, Michael Klim, Susan O'Neill

Tennis
Evonne Goolagong, Margaret Court, Rod Laver, Pat Cash, Pat Rafter, Lleyton Hewitt, The 'Woodies' (Mark Woodforde, Todd Woodbridge), Nick Kyrgios

V8s should check out the race at Bathurst, west of Sydney, every October. Phillip Island hosts the Australian Motorcycle Grand Prix and World Superbike Championships.

ENTERTAINMENT

Australia hosts the planet's best performers when they tour, and produces more than its share of world-class acts. Open any major city newspaper for advertised

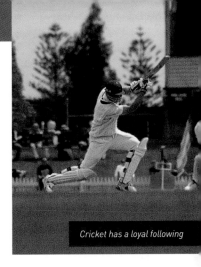

Cricket has a loyal following

performances of chamber music, opera, avant-garde plays, Aboriginal dance, comedy, cabaret, Shakespearean classics, rock concerts, Broadway hits, ballet, art shows and touring exhibitions from the top galleries of Europe and North America.

Australia's two largest cities, Sydney and Melbourne, present the greatest number of cultural events, but Adelaide stages the most extensive and exciting arts event – the Adelaide Festival (www.adelaidefestival.com.au) – held biennially on even-numbered years. Look out too for the annual Adelaide Fringe Festival (www.adelaidefringe.com.au).

Melbourne is famous for its vibrant live music and comedy scene, but Sydney, Brisbane and Perth all have good venues too. In some smaller towns, odd events such as cane-toad racing, thong throwing (an open-toed sandal is hurled as far as possible) and brick-throwing draw the crowds. In coastal towns and cities, summer surf carnivals are another favourite – a chance for lifeguards to show off their skills, as well as a celebration of Australian beach culture.

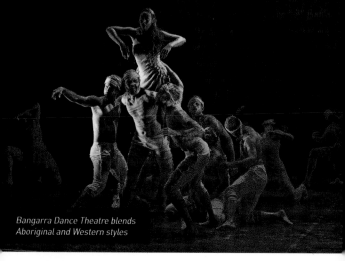

Bangarra Dance Theatre blends
Aboriginal and Western styles

On stage

Theatre has been going strong in Australia for a couple of centuries. In 1789, scarcely a year after New South Wales was founded, a troupe of convicts in Sydney put on a Restoration comedy *(The Recruiting Officer)* by George Farquhar as part of the celebrations for the birthday of King George III. The Theatre Royal, built in Hobart in 1834, is Australia's oldest. Sir Laurence Olivier described it as 'the best little theatre in the world'. Drama today is at its liveliest in Sydney and Melbourne but you can enjoy performances in most cities.

Opera has attracted keen audiences down under since the days of Dame Nellie Melba. In more recent times, the coloratura brilliance of Dame Joan Sutherland spread her fame around the world. Grand opera in the Sydney Opera House is a gala occasion; but opera-goers in other cities may enjoy better acoustics and atmosphere in their newer theatres.

Ballet and dance. The country's leading classical dance company, the Australian Ballet, founded in 1962, is based in Melbourne but performs in Sydney as well. Leading modern dance troupes include the Sydney Dance Company, the Australian Dance Theatre and the Bangarra Dance Theatre.

Music

Every state and territory in Australia has its own symphony orchestra; many maintain youth and chamber orchestras as well. An influential promoter of serious music, Musica Viva (www.musicaviva.com.au) presents thousands of concerts each year across the country. Sydney holds free – and hugely popular – open-air opera and classical concerts each year in the Domain as part of the Sydney Festival (www.sydneyfestival.org.au).

Jazz clubs exist in all the big cities, where you might hear a visiting celebrity or an up-and-coming local band. Plenty of pubs feature jazz, but usually at weekends only. Both indoor and outdoor jazz concerts are also advertised.

Other music – pop, rock, folk or rap – can reveal something of a nation's soul. Aussie options range from bearded troubadours dishing out bush ballads in Outback saloons to hard-hitting metal bands. Contemporary groups and individuals such as Courtney Barnett, Nick Cave and the Badseeds, The Living End, Banoffee and The Vines follow in the wake of past notables like the Seekers, the Bee Gees, Men at Work, INXS, Midnight Oil, AC/DC and Cold Chisel.

Nightlife

The scale and sophistication of an evening's entertainment depends on the size of the town. You won't find Jennifer Lopez or Sir Elton John performing in Burrumbuttock, New South Wales, but nightlife in Australia's smaller towns and remoter areas can still be a load of fun, as anyone who has attended an Outback bush dance or seen the Australian movie *The Adventures of Priscilla, Queen of the Desert* will know.

In larger centres and cities, nightlife venues, acts and attractions are listed in guides published in the daily newspapers, usually on Thursdays or Fridays. Posters slapped on walls and telegraph poles proclaim dance parties, gigs, plays and concerts.

Cinema

Nicole Kidman, Cate Blanchett, Geoffrey Rush, Mel Gibson, Hugh Jackman and Russell Crowe are probably Australia's best-known contemporary film stars. Other cinematic high fliers include Naomi Watts, Toni Collette, Rachel Griffiths, David Gulpilil, Sam Worthington, Bryan Brown, Deborah Mailman, Guy Pearce, Eric Bana and the great swashbuckler Errol Flynn, who hailed from Tasmania.

The Australian music scene is both vibrant and varied

Founded at the end of the 19th century, the Australian film industry took a great leap forward in the 1970s and has never really looked back. Films such as *Picnic at Hanging Rock*, *My Brilliant Career*, *Breaker Morant*, the *Mad Max* series and *Crocodile Dundee* – as well as the more off-beat *Strictly Ballroom*, *Muriel's Wedding* and *The Adventures of Priscilla, Queen of the Desert* – have given audiences around the world a glimpse of Australia's scenery and insight into the national character. More recently *Rabbit-Proof Fence*, *Ten Canoes*, *Wolf Creek*, *Chopper*, *Happy Feet*, *Australia*, and *The Sapphires* have also excelled. In recent years, many Australian actors have been critically acclaimed, from Geoffrey Rush and Heath Ledger to Jacki Weaver and Naomi Watts. In 2014, Cate Blanchett won Best Actress for her role in *Blue Jasmine* (her second statue, having previously won Best Supporting Actress for *The Aviator*), and in 2017 the film *Lion* was nominated for several Oscars; previous winner Nicole Kidman was once again nominated for her supporting role in the movie.

Multi-screen cinema complexes are popular in town centres as well as suburbs. Big cities also have specialised cinemas showing art films, foreign films and revivals. Film festivals are held annually in Sydney, Melbourne, Brisbane, Perth and Adelaide, showcasing both Australian-made movies and the best new films selected from international film festivals. Tropfest (www.tropfest.com), held annually at venues around the country, is the world's biggest short film festival.

SHOPPING

In most cities, the browsers and window-shoppers congregate along the pedestrian malls. Department-store chains David Jones and Myer provide a dependable cross-section of what's available. Downtown arcades and courts have smaller boutiques handling everything from high fashion to silly souvenirs.

In Sydney the Queen Victoria Building by Town Hall station is a great place to browse. In Melbourne the main shopping streets are Collins and Bourke, along with Bourke Street Mall, but the city's reputation as a shopping mecca owes plenty to the boutiques of South Yarra, Prahran and Brunswick, and the factory outlets of Richmond and beyond. Rundle Mall is the essence of shopping in Adelaide, and traffic-free Hay Street Mall is Perth's equivalent.

The state capitals are home to general **markets**, where stall-holders sell everything from clothing, jewellery and craftware to paintings, antiques and books. They are usually staged at weekends. Examples include Sydney's Paddington, Melbourne's Queen Victoria, Hobart's Salamanca and Darwin's Mindil Beach Sunset Markets – each with its own distinctive goods and atmosphere. If you are visiting country towns, keep an eye out for notices advertising markets.

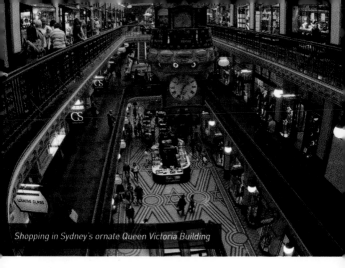
Shopping in Sydney's ornate Queen Victoria Building

These can be great places to absorb local atmosphere, find unusual offerings, and, perhaps, pick up a bargain.

Shopping hours usually run Monday to Friday from 8.30 or 9am to 5 or 5.30pm, and to 5pm on Saturdays in major towns and cities. One night a week, either Thursday or Friday depending on the city, stores stay open until 9pm or thereabouts. In larger cities, tourist needs are catered for on Sundays as well.

While shopping, keep in mind that overseas visitors are allowed to claim back the 10 percent GST (goods and services tax) added to all purchases (see page 242).

Aboriginal arts and crafts

The best places to find authentic boomerangs, didgeridoos and works of art are the Northern Territory and North Queensland, but you can find Aboriginal products in speciality stores all over the country. Outback artists produce traditional paintings on bark, the subjects and style recalling the prehistoric rock paintings featuring kangaroos, emus, crocodiles, snakes, fish and impressions of tribal ceremonies. Other indigenous painters use modern materials to produce canvases in a style that looks uncannily like some abstract-expressionist work, yet recounting Dreamtime legends and rituals. Though the themes are old, the economics are contemporary: the price tags on paintings may go into four or even five figures.

Fine workmanship is also seen on some of the painted wood sculptures of animals and birds. You'll see large, brightly decorated didgeridoos – wind instruments made from tree trunks hollowed out by obliging termites. Slightly easier to transport are clap-sticks for percussion accompaniment. Some Aboriginal craftsmen also produce decorated wooden shields and, rather inevitably, boomerangs. Baskets and tablemats woven from pandanus leaves are perhaps easier to carry home.

A word of warning: fakes and kitsch are sometimes represented as Aboriginal art by unscrupulous traders. To help identify genuine Aboriginal and Torres Strait Islander art, cultural products and services, Aboriginal communities have developed the Label of Authenticity, which employs the Aboriginal colours black, red and yellow and is protected by law.

Art and antiques

Paintings and prints by contemporary Australian artists are on show in commercial galleries in many areas, but the biggest concentration is in the big cities. Sydney galleries are clustered in the central shopping district and in Paddington. In Melbourne visit the City, Toorak Road and High Street, Armadale. They'll handle the packing, insurance and shipping details for you.

Antiques include some worthy colonial pieces: furniture, clocks, jewellery, porcelain, silverware, glassware and maps. Some dealers specialise in non-Australian antiques, for instance Chinese ceramics or Japanese screens. In Sydney, the Woollahra district is full of antiques shops. Melbourne's antiques centre is High Street, Armadale.

Huon pine, a slow-growing conifer unique to Tasmania, has long attracted the attention of wood-carvers. The timber, which is heavy, fine-grained and perfumed, is carved into furniture, salad bowls, egg-cups, candlesticks and even hair-curlers – be sure to buy from a reputable source, however, as 85 percent of Huon Pine is protected in Tasmania's National Forest, and only wood sourced from the remaining 15 percent should be sold.

Clothing

The **fashion** season just ending in Australia is always about to begin north of the equator – so Australian end-of-season sales can deliver excellent bargains that are instantly wearable upon your return home. 'Wearable art' in swimwear, fashion garments, fabrics and souvenirs proliferates. Names to look for include Ken Done, Leona Edmiston, Balarinji Australia, Country Road, Covers, Trent Nathan, Saba, Lisa Ho, Hussy, Studibaker Hawk, Perri Cutten, Von Troska, Alannah Hill, Trelise Cooper, Scanlan & Theodore, Morrissey, Zimmerman Wear and Carla Zampatti.

Elaborately painted didgeridoos for sale in Cairns

A distinct style of **Outback clothing** has evolved from rural Australia, the area collectively known as 'The Bush'. Driza-bone oilskin raincoats, Akubra hats (wide-brimmed hats usually made of felt) and the R.M. Williams range of bush wear (including boots and moleskin trousers) are good examples. Consider buying a pair of Blundstone boots, designed in Tasmania and renowned for their durability.

Sheepskin. In a country where sheep outnumber people by seven to one, sheep products are put to good use. Their hides are manufactured into a wide range of items. If it isn't too hot to think about it, you can choose from sheepskin boots, hats, coats, rugs and novelty items.

Woollen goods. It's those sheep again. Look for high-quality sweaters, scarves and shawls, and tapestries, too. You can also buy hand-spun wool. Australian merino sheep produce fine fleece ideally suited for spinning. All kinds of knitwear, from vivid children's clothing to Jumbuk brand greasy wool sweaters (which retain their natural water resistance) are available.

Precious stones

Australia is the source of about 95 percent of the world's **opals**. 'White' opals are mined from the fields of Andamooka and Coober Pedy in South Australia, where inhabitants live underground to escape searing summer heat. 'Boulder' opals – bright and vibrant – come from Quilpie in Queensland, while the precious 'black' opal (actually more blue than black) is mined at Lightning Ridge and White Cliffs in New South Wales. Opals, considered among Australia's best buys, are sold unset or as finished jewellery. Larger jewellery shops can arrange duty-free purchase for foreign visitors, but you may have to pay duty when you arrive home.

After opals, **sapphires** are Australia's most-mined gemstones. A sapphire is exactly the same stone as a ruby – the only difference is the name and the colour. Creative Australian jewellers work wonders with sapphires.

Souvenirs in Brisbane

Australia is one of the world's largest diamond sources. The Kimberley is famed for its 'pink' diamonds, sometimes marketed under the description 'champagne'. Hues range from lightly flushed to deep red.

Souvenirs

Souvenirs, whether ingenious or hackneyed, indigenous or imported, pop up everywhere you travel: in cities, resorts and at roadside stands. Tourists seem unable to resist miniature kangaroos, koalas and, in Tasmania, almost-lovable Tassie devil dolls.

Boomerangs and beer can–holders head the very long list of less artistic souvenirs, followed by saucy T-shirts. In Sydney, you'll find them cheap at Paddy's Market. In Melbourne, try Queen Victoria Market.

Kangaroo-skin souvenirs include toy kangaroos and koalas, wallets, purses, coin bags and keycases, and other such products – some of them quite trite. The cheapest of them, often wrapped in patriotic Australian packaging, are imported.

CALENDAR OF EVENTS

January

Australian Tennis Open: Grand Slam event at Melbourne Park.

Country Music Festival: Tamworth, New South Wales.

Hobart Taste Festival: one-week celebration of culture and food, beginning late December.

Perth Cup: horse racing classic at Royal Ascot Racecourse.

Port Lincoln Tunarama Festival: on the foreshore of Boston Bay, South Australia (includes the world tuna-throwing championships).

Sydney Festival: a month of music, dance, theatre and the visual arts.

February

Adelaide Festival of Arts (even-numbered years): three weeks of opera, ballet, theatre, art and literary events.

Launceston Cup: the social event of Tasmania.

Perth Festival: sporting and cultural events.

Sydney Gay and Lesbian Mardi Gras Parade: fun-filled, provocative parade along Oxford Street.

March–April

Australian Grand Prix: Formula 1 racing at Albert Park, Melbourne.

Canberra National Multicultural Festival.

Melbourne International Comedy Festival: world-class comedy acts at various venues

Moomba Waterfest, Melbourne: carnival with fireworks, music, river pageants and a street parade.

South Australia Vintage Festival, Barossa Valley (odd-numbered years): celebrating the wine harvest with German-Australian gaiety.

Sydney Royal Easter Show, at Olympic Park.

Ten Days on the Island (odd-numbered years), Tasmania: celebrating all that is Tassie.

WOMADelaide: Australian and international artists take part in this world music festival held in Adelaide.

May

Australian Celtic Festival, New South Wales: dancing, singing and art.

Barossa Valley Balloon Regatta: Nuriootpa in the Barossa Valley.

Biennale of Sydney (even-numbered years): visual arts festival

June–July

Bounty Day, Norfolk Island: 8 June (anniversary of the Bounty mutineers' arrival in 1856), festivities culminate in a Bounty Ball.

Brisbane Cup: horse race.

Cairns Adventure Festival: An Ironman, plus on and off-road races for runners, bike riders and swimmers.

Camel Cup: camel racing at Blatherskite Park, Alice Springs.

Darwin Beer Can Regatta: all the boats constructed of used beer cans.

Gold Coast Marathon: Queensland.

Royal Darwin Show: agricultural exhibition.

Sydney Film Festival.

Taste of Manly: annual food and wine festival.

August–September

Australian Masters Alpine Ski Races: Snowy Mountains.

Australian Motorcycle Grand Prix: Phillip Island, Victoria.

Birdsville Races, Queensland: a weekend of horse racing and revelry.

Carnival of Flowers: Toowoomba, Queensland.

Floriade, Canberra: Australia's biggest flower show.

Henley-on-Todd Regatta, Alice Springs: dry-land bottomless boat race.

Jabiru Wind Festival: cultural community event in Kakadu National Park.

Mount Isa Rodeo and Festival, Queensland: Australia's biggest rodeo.

Royal Adelaide Show: South Australia's agricultural summit meeting.

Royal Melbourne Show: bucolic and sporting attractions.

Royal Queensland Show, Brisbane: agricultural fair with fireworks.

October

Melbourne International Arts Festival: visual and performing arts.

Royal Hobart Agricultural Show: Tasmania's agricultural highlight.

November

Melbourne Cup: one of the world's premier horse-racing events.

December

Sydney–Hobart: one of the world's toughest yacht races.

Various capital cities: New Year's Eve celebrations with fireworks. Western Australian Turf Club Derby: horse racing.

EATING OUT

If you enjoy perusing a wide choice of menus reflecting varied ethnic influences, you're going to enjoy eating in Australia's cities – but you'll pay handsomely for it too. The cost of eating and drinking out in Australia has sadly soared in the last decade, but if your budget allows you can enjoy genuinely world-class cuisine, particularly seafood.

All state capitals have a lively café and restaurant scene in their inner-city areas. While restaurant meals are expensive and bar prices high, you can pick up reasonably priced meals from a variety of places, particularly if you enjoy Asian cuisine. Trendy street eats (pop-ups and food vans) are also good to explore, and the coffee culture rivals – actually, surpasses – that of Italy.

Many restaurants permit you to BYO ('bring your own') wine, allowing you to take along store-bought wine to enjoy with your meal. A small 'corkage' fee usually applies, but this can save you a substantial amount of money. Shop-bought, Australian wine is relatively inexpensive and of high quality.

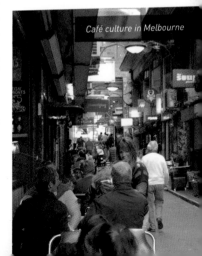

Café culture in Melbourne

Australian cooks have the advantage of the availability of a wonderful palette of ingredients. The country's climatic diversity provides a wide range of fresh vegetables and fruits, ranging from exotic rambutans, coconuts and lychees to apples, pears and spinach.

This culinary wonderland has developed gradually over the last three decades. During most of the two centuries of modern Australia's existence, its inhabitants subsisted on bland 'meat and veg' fodder, in which lamb chops and three vegetables were standard fare. Cultural intermingling since World War II has revolutionised the national diet. Urban Australia now eats what has been described as 'fusion food' – a collage of culinary influences, embracing European and Asian influences, that enlivens basic fish,

⊙ INDIGENOUS CUISINE

Recent innovations by Australian chefs have included greater use of indigenous foods in fine dining. Lemon aspen, bush tomatoes, Illawarra plums, lemon myrtle, lilli pillies, muntari berries and other mysterious ingredients are now appearing on menus, often blended with traditional dishes of meat and fish. Kangaroo and emu are commercially farmed and processed. (Both meats are low in fat and high in protein.) Collectively known as native food – or sometimes bush tucker – these are just some of the fruits, seeds, nuts, fungi, mammals, reptiles, fish and birds that sustained Australia's indigenous inhabitants for up to 100,000 years before white settlers came to the region.

Other bush-tucker ingredients include quandongs (similar to a peach with a touch of rhubarb), wattle seeds (sometimes used in ice cream), Kakadu plums (less sweet than the usual variety) and bunya bunya nuts (delicious in satay). Even wilder Aboriginal ingredients, very rarely seen in restaurants, include the Bogong moth (a hefty moth roasted in a fire and eaten like a peanut) and the witchetty grub (a puffy, white grub found in the trunks and roots of certain wattle trees), which has been shown to be a virtual powerhouse of protein.

Seafood-lovers are spoilt for choice in Australia

grain or meat with, for example, a handful of chopped coriander, a splash of olive oil and a dash of chilli.

If you're into exotic fare, sample goat cheeses from Western Australia or Victoria, cold-pressed olive oils from South Australia, buffalo mozzarella from New South Wales, barramundi fish from the Northern Territory, or oysters, scallops, salmon and other sea-food ingredients from Tasmania's waters.

Fine-dining options are generally restricted to inner-city areas and some wine-producing regions, but most suburbs and country towns have at least one decent Thai or Chinese restaurant. There are, however, culinary black holes, especially in remote rural areas, where café menus will probably include nothing more exotic than spaghetti Bolognese. The traditional Aussie meat pie, doused liberally with tomato sauce, rules supreme in these out-posts, as does the hamburger (always with a slice of beetroot, and sometimes with pineapple and a fried egg for good measure). The standard US fast-food chains also litter the nation's suburbs and country towns.

WHAT TO EAT

Breakfast is anything you want it to be, from muesli and grapes or coffee and croissant to a typical English breakfast. It depends on where you are and your hunger level. If you are really hungry, some establishments will serve you a breakfast based on steak or lamb chops with eggs. Try Vegemite on toast – it's a rite of passage for visitors to Australia, but don't go too heavy with the spread.

Fish and seafood. From traditional fish and chips eaten standing up, to lobster savoured by candlelight, Australia's temperate and tropical oceans offer a fantastic choice of seafood. Fish adorning the menu include the delicious snapper, the meaty John Dory, smallish flounder and bigger sole, the bony but flavoursome whiting (no relation to the English whiting), the tropical trevally and 'flake' – a generic term for shark. Then there's barramundi, which means 'big scales' in an Aboriginal language, and is found in both fresh and salt water; game fishermen in the north take 'barra' of up to 15kg (33lb). Along the Great Barrier Reef they even eat red emperor, a fish so gorgeous it might take a snorkeller's breath away.

Treat yourself to succulent seafood specialities such as Sydney rock oysters (as delicious as any in the world), Brisbane's famous Moreton Bay bug (a crustacean that tastes a lot better than it looks), and gloriously meaty mud crabs. Lobster, grilled or thermidor, is priced for special occasions. You are also likely to come across some of the lobster's freshwater cousins, small crayfish known locally as yabbies. Prices are less forbidding when it comes to steamed mussels or prawns. A popular and simple Australian alfresco meal for two consists of a kilo (2.2lb) of prawns and a bottle of ice-cold white wine. Scrumptious!

Meat favourites include steak and roast lamb, particularly in simpler restaurants, and pork is also popular. Good-quality organic meats are now on offer at many city and country restaurants. Meat pies are a long-established staple; in Adelaide the speciality is the

Delicious waffles for dessert

'floater', a pie served floating in pea soup. If you're feeling adventurous, you can dine on Australian fauna, such as kangaroo, crocodile or emu; all three are healthy alternatives to the usual fare. The feral camel, too, has found its way onto plates in the Red Centre, and is very tasty.

Vegetables are available in as much variety as anywhere else in the world. As with meat, organic vegetables are on the rise. In restaurants, either vegetables or a salad may accompany your main course, but note that there is a trend for city restaurants to charge extra for these 'sides'.

Fruit in Australia covers all the climatic zones, from the familiar (apples, pears, cherries, plums and berries from the temperate latitudes) to the tropical (avocados, bananas, papayas, passion fruit, pineapples, lychees, rambutans and mangoes).

Desserts. If you have a sweet tooth, you'll be in your element here, as there are any number of dessert to dive into, from light fruit-based offerings to heavy puddings. A traditional Australian favourite is the light and fluffy pavlova, a meringue concoction traditionally topped with fresh cream and fruit. It's a common home-cooked desert, but worth sampling if you see it on a menu. Peach Melba, created for Melbourne's famous opera singer Nellie Melba by the great French chef Escoffier, is still sometimes found on dessert menus. Also look for ice cream flavoured with wattle seed – roasted ground acacia seeds – which tastes a bit like coffee, and macadamia nuts.

Sydney stalwart Bar Coluzzi

EXOTIC IMPORTS

The massive migration from Mediterranean countries – mainly Italy and Greece – after World War II made the first real dent in Australia's monolithic Anglo-Saxon palate. Italians in particular helped revolutionise cooking, introducing wary Aussies to the wonders of pasta, garlic and olive oil. Today, each capital city has its concentration of Italian restaurants – Melbourne's Lygon Street in the suburb of Carlton and Sydney's Norton Street in Leichhardt being the most famous – serving authentic, well-priced food. In Melbourne, with its large Greek population, it is easy to find traditionally made *taramasalata, dolmades* or *souvlaki*.

But that was only the beginning. The extension of immigration in the 1970s added myriad new cuisines. The great melting-pot of Australian society meant that restaurants were suddenly opened by Lebanese, Turkish, Balkan, Hungarian and Spanish chefs.

The biggest recent influence has come from Asia. Regional Chinese, Thai, Vietnamese, Japanese and Indian restaurants are now Australia's biggest success stories, with Korean, Sri Lankan,

Singaporean and Indonesian cuisines waiting in the wings. Every capital city offers *teppanyaki* dining rooms and take-away *laksa* stalls. Singapore-style 'food courts' have sprung up, which have several fast-food stalls offering meals from different Asian cuisines. Supermarkets stock the required pastes and condiments for everyone's favourite Thai or Indian dish.

AUSTRALIAN WINES

The wines of Australia are among the world's best – a judgment confirmed consistently at international wine shows. Not only are the country's finest wines world-beaters, but even the humble 'kangarouge' sold in boxes ('casks') is the worthy equivalent of any *vin de table* served in a bistro in France. Australians drink more than twice as much wine per capita as Americans, and anything that's left over (800 million litres of it) is exported to over 100 countries. Wine is one of the country's most important export industries and the range sold in liquor stores is extensive and moderately priced.

Australia's interest in wine production stretches back a couple of centuries. The founder of the New South Wales colony, Captain Arthur Phillip, certainly had his priorities right, and one of the first projects he ordered in 1788 was the planting of vines at Sydney Cove. But the site (now part of Sydney's Botanic Gardens) was quite wrong for growing grapes, and the experiment failed.

Rum, rather than wine, became the favourite drink under Governor Phillip's successor. Free-enterprising army officers enjoyed a monopoly on the staggeringly profitable sales of rum, and widespread abuses were reported to London. It was Captain William Bligh, the original hardliner of *Bounty* fame, who was dispatched to clean up Australia. Governor Bligh was deposed in the Rum Rebellion of 1808, a mutiny led by one of the first wine-growers, John Macarthur.

Today, most of Australia's European grape varieties are grown by some 2,000 wine producers on 152,000 hectares (376,000 acres) of vineyards. Riesling, Chardonnay and Semillon are the most favoured white varieties, while popular reds include Cabernet Sauvignon, Pinot Noir and Shiraz (also known in Europe as Syrah). Climatic conditions ranging from warm to hot provide excellent ripening, with an abundance of flavour and comparatively high sugar levels. Australia's vintage (harvest) occurs between January and May each year.

Wine is produced in every state. The biggest producer is South Australia, where the best-known wineries are situated in the beautiful Barossa Valley, famed for its Shiraz. The most important wine-producing region of New South Wales is the Hunter Valley, noted for its Semillon and Shiraz. Victoria boasts numerous wine-growing regions (the Yarra Valley and Mornington Peninsula are the closest to Melbourne and specialise in cool-climate varieties), and Western Australia's Swan Valley and Margaret River areas have also made their mark with excellent Cabernets and Chardonnays. Tasmania's temperate climate produces some fine Pinot Noir.

If you're interested in seeing where the wine comes from, every state capital has wine-growing areas nearby, and the chance to sample wines at the cellar door is one of their most interesting features. As most wineries are concentrated in a relatively small area, they make ideal touring for a day or – better still – two days, either independently or on a guided tour.

THE AMBER NECTAR

During the 19th century, most Australian beer was made like English ales, until, just over 100 years ago, German immigrants began to brew lighter Continental-style lagers in Melbourne. Nowadays lager is the dominant style, and it's hugely popular throughout the country.

Beer is served very cold. Temperature is considered so important that beer-lovers will insist on chilled glasses, or will keep their 'tinnie' (can) or 'stubbie' (short bottle) in an insulating jacket.

Internationally the best-known Aussie beer is probably Foster's lager, but you rarely see that on tap in Australia. More popular are brews such as Carlton Draught, Tooheys New, Victoria Bitter, XXXX (pronounced Four X), Cascade and Boags. Some beers are sold in 'new' and 'old' types, the first being lager and the latter darker in colour – approaching a stout. Coopers Sparkling Ale made in South Australia, is a favourite among connoisseurs – it's rich and strong, similar to the best British real ales. In the last decade there has been a craft beer revolution in Australia, with boutique breweries such as Little Creatures, Matilda Bay, Fat Yak and Mountain Goat producing some very fine ales.

Beer is bought in a confusing mixture of measures that vary from state to state. Typically you will be served a 'schooner' (around 450ml) in Sydney and a 'pot' (285ml) in Melbourne. Many places serve jugs (1140ml) and pints (sometimes 500ml, sometimes 570ml). In Adelaide, a schooner-sized glass is referred to as a 'pint'. One thing you can be reasonable sure of, is that you will pay a hefty price for whatever size glass you order – the average cost of a pint is currently around A\$7. Beer from bottleshops (some of which offer a drive-through service) is considerably cheaper.

Australia's standard alcoholic strength for canned beer is 4.9 percent – pretty strong by international standards. A word of advice for weight-watchers from Europe or America: the word 'light' or 'lite' applied to beer in Australia means lighter in alcohol, not much lighter in calories. The alcoholic strength of beer is displayed on the can or bottle.

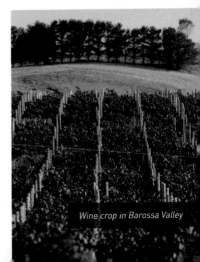

Wine crop in Barossa Valley

A–Z TRAVEL TIPS

A SUMMARY OF PRACTICAL INFORMATION

A Accommodation _____ 225
Airports _____ 226

B Bicycle hire _____ 226
Budgeting for
your trip _____ 227

C Camping _____ 228
Car hire _____ 228
Climate _____ 229
Clothing _____ 230
Crime and safety _____ 230

D Driving _____ 231

E Electricity _____ 234
Embassies/
consulates/high
commissions _____ 234
Emergencies _____ 235

G Gay and lesbian
travellers _____ 235
Getting to Australia _____ 235
Guides and tours _____ 236

H Health and
medical care _____ 237

M Maps _____ 239
Media _____ 239
Money _____ 239

N National parks _____ 240

O Opening hours _____ 241

P Police _____ 241
Post offices _____ 241
Public holidays _____ 242

R Religion _____ 242

T Tax refunds _____ 242
Telephones _____ 243
Time zones _____ 244
Tipping _____ 244
Toilets _____ 245
Tourist information _____ 245
Transport _____ 246

V Visas and entry
requirements _____ 247

W Websites and
internet access _____ 248

Y Youth hostels _____ 249

A

ACCOMMODATION (see also Camping, Youth Hostels)

Australia welcomes travellers with all kinds of accommodation. The luxury end of the spectrum matches the most sumptuous world standards, in the rooms and suites as well as the associated restaurants, lounges, saunas and spas. But even in budget-priced hotel and motel rooms you can expect a private shower/bath and toilet, a telephone, a TV set, a small refrigerator and coffee- and tea-making equipment (along with free coffee, tea and milk). In most regions, air-conditioning, or at least a ceiling fan, is provided.

There's no limit to the level of luxury a hotel or motel can attain. Distinguishing between the two can be confusing. The only sure difference is that a hotel has a bar open to the public – indeed, the most modest ones have little else to offer. To add to the confusion, 'hotel' is also a synonym for 'pub' here.

Private hotels, often small guesthouses, do not have a licence for alcohol. Bed-and-breakfast establishments – private homes taking paying guests – exist in towns or out on the farms. Big towns and resorts, and even some parks, also offer self-catering apartments with fully equipped kitchens, convenient for longer stays.

Overseas offices of Tourism Australia have listings of hotels and motels – see www.australia.com. You can reserve accommodation directly or through your travel agent, airline or web-based intermediaries. Within Australia, the state tourist bureau, domestic airlines and hotel chains offer booking services. If you arrive out of the blue, local tourist offices have desks for last-minute reservations.

Accommodation may be hard to find when Australians themselves go travelling en masse, during school holidays. These can vary, but most states have adopted a four-term school year with two-week breaks in April, June/July and September/October. The Christmas/summer holidays are from mid-December to the beginning of February.

AIRPORTS

The main gateways are **Adelaide** (ADL; www.adelaideairport.com.au), **Brisbane** (BNE; www.bne.com.au), **Cairns** (CNS; www.cairnsairport. com), **Darwin** (DIA; www.darwinairport.com.au), **Melbourne** (MEL; www.melbourneairport.com.au), **Perth** (PER; www.perthairport.com) and **Sydney** (SYD; www.sydneyairport.com.au). Other international airports serve Townsville, Canberra and Hobart. The domestic air network is very well developed, and even smallish towns usually have comfortable, efficient terminals.

Arriving passengers can travel from airport to town by taxi or bus. In Sydney, Brisbane, Adelaide, Darwin and Perth, airport bus services go to and from the door of most hotels. Travel time ranges from 20 minutes (Perth and Darwin) to 40 minutes (Sydney). Note that Sydney Airport's domestic and international terminals are a shuttle-bus ride apart. There are also rail links between Sydney and Brisbane airports and their respective CBDs. Typical taxi fares from Sydney and Melbourne airports to the CBD vary between A$40 and A$60.

Check-in time for departing passengers on domestic flights is one hour before the scheduled flight time; international flights require check-in at least two hours in advance.

B

BICYCLE HIRE

Most Australian cities are reasonably attuned to cyclists, and bicycle lanes are sometimes marked on inner-city streets. Cycling in Canberra is excellent, and the flatness of Melbourne and Adelaide make those cities popular with cyclists. Cars clog most large cities, however, and attempts to cater for cyclists are often little more than cosmetic. Road rage can certainly be directed towards cyclists. Throughout Australia, cyclists must wear helmets at all times by law.

Organised cycle tours of varying lengths are available, including transport to and from a scenic area (bikes provided), food and accommodation (Tasmania is a popular bike-touring destination). You can also rent touring bikes. For details, look up 'Bicycles & Accessories on www.yellowpages.com.au.

Cycling organisations, such as those following, are a good source of information:

Bicycle Network Australia: tel: 02-6249 6761; www.bicycles.net.au
Pedal Power ACT (Canberra): tel: 02-6248 7995; www.pedalpower.org.au
Bicycle New South Wales: tel: 02-9704 0800; www.bicyclensw.org.au
Bicycle Queensland: tel: 07-3844 1144; www.bq.org.au
Bicycle South Australia: tel: 08-8168 9999; www.bikesa.asn.au
Bicycle Tasmania: tel: 0475 803 663; www.biketas.org.au
Bicycle Victoria: tel: 03-8376 8888; www.bv.com.au

BUDGETING FOR YOUR TRIP

You can eat out well for little money (so long as you don't want a beer): a plate of noodles or pasta can cost about A$15. Accommodation also represents good value when measured against equivalents in other developed countries. Budget accommodation starts at A$30 for a dorm bed and A$70 for an ensuite double room. Comfortable B&Bs and well-appointed hotel rooms start at around A$130 a double.

As far as domestic air travel is concerned, Qantas (www.qantas.com.au) is the major player, but you should be able to find cheaper fares – and some bargains – with the budget airlines, Virgin Australia (www.virginaustralia.com), Jetstar (www.jetstar.com) and Tigerair (www.tigerair.com). International passengers may be entitled to discounted travel within Australia, depending on the airline they arrive on and their fare type.

On the ground, train travel can be competitive for shorter distances, and budget long-distance coach operations abound. Inner city buses are very cheap and easy to use.

In 2017, the cost of a litre of petrol (gasoline) was approximately A$1.30 – cheaper than in the majority of European countries.

C

CAMPING (see also Car hire and National parks)

Australians are avid campers, and you'll find campgrounds dotted all over the areas frequented by tourists. Campgrounds tend to be jam-packed at school holiday times. They have at least the basic amenities, and in some cases much more in the way of comfort. Apart from powered and unpowered sites for pitching a tent or parking a campervan, some campgrounds have caravans (trailers) or cabins for rent. Showers, toilets, laundry facilities and barbecue grills are commonly available.

The national parks generally have well-organised camping facilities; to camp beyond the designated zone you must ask the rangers for permission. There are coach tours for campers, or you can rent a camper van or motorhome by the day or week.

CAR HIRE (see also Driving)

For seeing the Australian countryside at your own pace, there's no substitute for a car. Brisk competition among the international and local car hire companies means you can often find economical rates or special deals, for instance unlimited mileage or weekend discounts. Rates are considerably higher if you drive in remote country areas. In general, it's worth shopping around. But be careful – some cheap companies impose a metropolitan limit on vehicles. Check first, as your insurance won't be valid outside the designated area.

In busy locations you can hire anything from a super-economy model (approximately A\$50 per day), medium-sized car (A\$80) or a four-wheel-drive vehicle (A\$250 per day). Campervans and caravans are available, though many are reserved well in advance for school holiday periods.

To hire a car you'll need a current Australian, overseas or International driving licence. The minimum age is 21, or in some cases 25. Third-party insurance is automatically included, and for an additional fee you can also sign up for collision damage waiver and personal accident insurance.

You can pick up a car in one city and return it elsewhere (though often you'll pay for this privilege). Interstate arrangements are commonly available from the big firms like Avis (tel: 13 63 33; www.avis.com.au), Europcar (tel: 1300 131 390; www.europcar.com.au), Hertz (tel: 13 30 39; www.hertz.com.au), Thrifty (tel: 1300 367 227; www.thrifty.com.au) and Budget (tel: 1300 362 848; www.budget.com.au), which also have offices at airports.

CLIMATE

Travellers from the Northern Hemisphere find Australia's seasons upside down: winter runs from June to August and Christmas comes in summertime. But it's much more complicated than that, for Australia covers so much ground, from the tropics to the temperate zone.

From November to March it's mostly hot – or at least quite warm – everywhere. In the north this period brings high humidity and rain, which can wash out roads and otherwise spoil holiday plans. In the south the nights, at least, are normally mild. The period from April to September is generally ideal in the tropics and central Australia – clear and warm. Occasional rain refreshes the south, with snow in the southern mountains.

The table below gives the average daily maximum and minimum temperatures in degrees Fahrenheit. (Minimum temperatures are measured just before sunrise, maximum temperatures in the afternoon.)

°F		J	F	M	A	M	J	J	A	S	O	N	D
Sydney	max.	79	77	77	72	66	63	61	63	68	72	75	77
	min.	64	64	63	59	52	48	46	48	52	55	59	63
Brisbane	max.	84	84	82	79	73	71	68	72	75	79	82	84
	min.	69	68	66	61	55	52	48	50	55	61	64	63
Alice	max.	99	97	91	84	73	68	66	72	79	88	93	95
Springs	min.	72	71	64	57	48	43	41	45	50	59	64	68
Perth	max.	86	86	82	75	71	64	63	64	66	71	77	81
	min.	64	64	63	57	54	50	48	48	50	52	57	61

...and the same in degrees Celsius:

°C		J	F	M	A	M	J	J	A	S	O	N	D
Sydney	max.	26	25	25	22	19	17	16	17	20	22	24	25
	min.	18	18	17	15	11	9	8	9	11	13	15	17
Brisbane	max.	29	29	28	26	23	21	20	22	24	26	28	29
	min.	21	20	19	16	13	11	9	10	13	16	18	17
Alice	max.	37	36	33	29	23	20	19	22	26	31	34	35
Springs	min.	22	21	18	14	9	6	5	7	10	15	18	20
Perth	max.	30	30	28	24	21	18	17	18	19	21	25	27
	min.	18	18	17	14	12	10	9	9	10	11	14	16

CLOTHING

A sweater may come in handy, even in summer. After a hot day in the sun, the evening breeze can seem chilly. A light raincoat will serve in any season. Anywhere you go you'll need comfortable walking shoes. Because of the strong sun, a hat is advisable.

While Sydneysiders dress casually at weekends (shorts, a short-sleeved shirt or T-shirt and trainers or sandals are perfect), business attire can be surprisingly conservative. Visit any popular downtown pub in Sydney or Melbourne at lunchtime on a summer weekday and you encounter hundreds of men in dark blue suits and ties, trying to cope with the sweltering heat. Restaurants have dropped the requirement for men to wear jacket and tie, but some establishments may refuse customers wearing T-shirts, tank tops or ripped jeans. Entering clubs generally requires a collared shirt and covered shoes – no trainers, thongs (flip-flops) or sandals.

CRIME AND SAFETY (see also Emergencies)

As in most countries, it's wise to take precautions against burglary and petty theft. Check your valuables into the hotel's safe deposit box. Lock your room and your car. Be alert for pickpockets on crowded buses and in the markets.

Overall, Australia is a safe place. Sydney's murder rate (1 per 100,000 citizens) is low by world standards and the city, Australia's biggest, has a relatively low crime rate. The same is true of other Australian cities, although muggings and fights are not unknown. It's best to avoid city parks after dark, particularly if on your own. Anti-drug laws vary greatly from state to state. In NSW for example, the offence of possessing a prohibited drug carries a maximum penalty of two years imprisonment. There is a very long list of drugs that are illegal to possess. The most common examples include cannabis. Narcotics are treated much more severely. The emergency number is 000.

D

DRIVING (see also Car hire)

Road conditions. Australian roads are good considering the size of the country and the challenge distance, terrain and climate present. Freeways link populous regions, but most country roads are two-lane highways, which can be crowded at busy times. Outback roads are often unpaved and, in the tropical north, can be impassable during the wet season.

Rules and regulations. Australians drive on the left – which means the steering wheel is on the right, and you overtake on the right. Drivers and passengers must wear seat belts. (The exception is buses, although many of them feature seat belts as an option.) Car-hire companies can supply suitable child restraints, boosters and baby seats at an extra charge.

A tourist may drive in Australia on a valid overseas licence for the same class of vehicle. Licences must always be carried when driving. If the licence is in a language other than English, the visitor must carry a translation with the licence. An International Driver's Permit must be accompanied by a valid national driver's licence.

The speed limit in cities and towns is generally 50kmh (about 30mph), but many major suburban roads have a 60kmh (about 35mph) speed limit. Outside built-up areas the speed limit is generally either 100kmh or 110kmh (about 70mph). Speed limits are rigorously enforced with fixed and mobile cameras and radars.

Throughout Australia, police make random checks for drugs or alcohol, using breath and saliva tests. The limit on alcohol in the blood is 0.05 for holders of a full licence, meaning in practice that one or two glasses of wine or two or three half-pint glasses of beer in an hour will take you to the limit. Holders of provisional licences (including overseas licences) must observe a zero alcohol limit. In any state, being over the limit means an automatic hefty fine and worse.

Outback driving. Check thoroughly the condition of your car and be sure you have a spare tyre and plenty of drinking water. Find out about the fuel situation in advance and always be sure to leave word as to your destination and anticipated arrival time. Fill up the fuel tank at every opportunity, as the next station may be a few hundred kilometres away. Some dirt roads are so smooth you may be tempted to speed, but conditions can change abruptly. Be cautious when you encounter a 'road train' – a high-powered truck towing three or four trailers along the highway at speed. Pass only with the greatest of care.

Parking. Heavy traffic and parking problems afflict some downtown areas. Parking meters and 'no standing' zones are everywhere, so be careful where you leave the car.

If you need help. The Australian Automobile Association (www.aaa.asn. au) is a national body that maintains links with similar organisations worldwide. Many state automobile associations have reciprocal arrangements with similar organisations overseas, so bring proof of your membership.

New South Wales: NRMA, 9 York Street, Sydney, NSW 2000; tel: 132132; www.mynrma.com.au

Victoria: RACV, 550 Princes Highway, Noble Park, Victoria 3174; tel: 03-9790 2211; www.racv.com.au

Queensland: RACQ, 300 St Paul's Terrace, Fortitude Valley, QLD 4006; tel: 07-3845 4851 or 131905; www.racq.com.au

South Australia: RAA, 55 Hindmarsh Square, Adelaide, SA 5000; tel: 08-8202 4600; www.raa.com.au

Tasmania: RACT, Corner of Patrick and Murray Streets, Hobart, TAS 7000; tel: 13 27 22; www.ract.com.au

Western Australia: RACWA, 832 Wellington Street, West Perth WA 6000; tel: 131703; www.rac.com.au

Northern Territory: AANT, 79-81 Smith Street, Darwin, NT 0800; Tel: 08-8925 5901 or 131111; www.aant.com.au

Fuel. Some filling stations are open only during normal shopping hours, so you may have to ask where after-hours service is available. Petrol (gasoline) in Australia comes in regular and premium grades of unleaded, and is sold by the litre. Most stations also pump liquefied petroleum gas (LPG) and diesel. Stations are self-service and accept international credit cards.

Road signs. Signs are generally good, especially along heavily used roads. All distances are measured in kilometres. White-on-brown direction signs signal tourist attractions. To drive into the centre of any city, simply follow the signs marked 'City'. Leaving a city is less straightforward; exit routes are often signposted with the assumption that every driver has local experience, so you may require a map or GPS. Most road signs are the standard international pictographs, but some are unique to Australia, such as silhouette images of kangaroos or wombats, warning that you may encounter these animals crossing the road.

Some signs use words, such as:

Crest steep hilltop limiting visibility

Cyclist hazard dangerous for cyclists

Dip severe depression in road surface

Hump bump or speed obstacle

Safety ramp uphill escape lane from steep downhill road

E

ELECTRICITY

The standard voltage throughout Australia is 230–250 volt, 50-cycle AC. Three-pronged plugs, in the shape of a bird's footprint, are universal. They are the same as in New Zealand and many Pacific countries. If you have plugs from elsewhere, you will need an adapter. Many hotel rooms also have 110-volt outlets for razors and small appliances.

EMBASSIES/CONSULATES/HIGH COMMISSIONS

The embassies or high commissions of about 70 countries are established in Canberra, the national capital. They have consular sections dealing with passport renewal, visas and other formalities. Some of them run consular sections in Sydney and other cities, as well. To find the address of your consulate, check the internet or look in the white pages of the telephone directory under 'Consuls', or on the Yellow Pages website under 'Consulates and Legations'.

Following are some of Canberra's embassies and high commissions:

British High Commission: Commonwealth Avenue, Yarralumla, ACT 2600; tel: 02-6270 6666; www.gov.uk/government/world/australia

Canadian High Commission: Commonwealth Avenue, Yarralumla, ACT 2600; tel: 02-6270 4000; www.canadainternational.gc.ca/Australia-australie

Irish Embassy: 20 Arkana Street, Yarralumla, ACT 2600; tel: 02-6214 0000; www.embassyofireland.au.com

Japanese Embassy: 112 Empire Circuit, Yarralumla, ACT 2600; tel: 02-6273 3244; www.au.emb-japan.go.jp

New Zealand High Commission: Commonwealth Avenue, Yarralumla, ACT 2600; tel: 02-6270 4211; www.nzembassy.com/australia

South Africa High Commission: Corner of State Circle and Rhodes Place, Yarralumla, ACT 2600; tel: 02-6272 7300; www.sahc.org.au

United States Embassy: Moonah Place, Yarralumla, ACT 2600; tel: 02-6214 5600; http://canberra.usembassy.gov

EMERGENCIES

Ambulance/Fire/Police: dial 000.

The 000 number – free from public telephones – is in service in all cities and towns. You can also dial 112 if using a mobile phone.

In the big cities there are round-the-clock dental emergency services as well as hospital emergency wards.

G

GAY AND LESBIAN TRAVELLERS

Sydney's huge Gay and Lesbian Mardi Gras has helped make Sydney – and Australia – a popular destination for gay and lesbian travellers. Some tour operators, travel agents and hotels specialise in catering for a gay and lesbian clientele. Australian cities are generally tolerant towards gay and lesbian travellers but prejudice tends to increase in more remote, country areas. Male homosexual acts were illegal in Queensland until 1990, and there is still a discrepancy in the age of consent (16 for heterosexual relationships; 18 for homosexual) but homosexuality is now legal in all states and territories. Sydney is one of the world's major gay cities, sometimes called 'the gay capital of the Southern Hemisphere'. Sydney's main gay precinct is Oxford Street (sometimes called 'the Golden Mile') and the surrounding Darlinghurst and Surry Hills areas, with another precinct in King Street, Newtown.

GETTING TO AUSTRALIA

By air. Flights from Asia, North America and Europe serve international airports around Australia, principally Brisbane, Melbourne Sydney and Perth, but you can also fly directly to Cairns, Darwin, Hobart, Canberra or Adelaide from some international points. Sydney's airport is by far the busiest in the country. All Australian airports have high volumes of traffic around the Christmas holiday period, which coincides with the Australian midsummer. Fares are generally at their highest then, and flights are heavily booked in both directions.

More than 35 airlines fly to and from Australia, including Air Canada (www.aircanada.com); Air New Zealand (www.airnewzealand.com); American Airlines (www.aa.com); British Airways (www.britishairways.com); Cathay Pacific (www.cathaypacific.com); Emirates Airlines (www.emirates.com); Etihad Airways (www.etihadairways.com); Malaysia Airlines (www.malaysiaairlines.com); Qantas (www.qantas.com.au); Singapore Airlines (www.singaporeair.com); South African Airways (www.flysaa.com); Thai Airways (www.thaiair.com); United Airlines (www.united.com); Virgin Australia (www.virginaustralia.com).

Flight times to Sydney (approximate) are as follows: London–Sydney 21 hours, New York–Sydney 22 hours, Los Angeles–Sydney 15 hours. You can usually break the flight for a day or two at one of the stops along the way; in most cases this doesn't affect the price of the air ticket.

By sea. Some Australian ports, notably Sydney and Cairns, feature on the itineraries of cruise ships. You can fly to locales like Bali or Singapore and embark on the cruise liner there, sail to Australia, then fly home from any Australian city, or resume the cruise at another port. It tends to be an involved process, however. Travel agents have cruise line schedules and brochures.

If you have a few weeks or more up your sleeve, it's also possible to hitch a ride on a cargo ship to Australia from Europe, Asia and the Americas, see www.freighterexpeditions.com.au and www.cargoshipvoyages.com for more.

GUIDES AND TOURS

Tour companies offer a broad choice of excursions, from a day-trip around Canberra to bush-tucker excursions and long-haul journeys into the Outback. There are also local walking tours and tours for cyclists, wildlife-lovers and others catering for special interests. The best and most up-to-date information about these will come from other travellers – check online forums. Don't forget to ask about the typical age group of the other passengers – some companies specialise in the backpacker scene. The best tours are usually local-based specialists, but national tour companies can be convenient and include: AAT Kings (www.aatkings.com.au), Adventure Tour Australia (www.adventuretours.com.au). Or you can devise your own tour using a Greyhound bus pass (see www.greyhound.com.au)

H

HEALTH AND MEDICAL CARE

Standards of hygiene in Australia are high. Doctors and dentists are proficient and hospitals well equipped. If you fall ill, your hotel can call a doctor or refer you to one, or you can ask your embassy, high commission or consulate for a list of approved doctors.

You should take out health insurance before departure to cover your stay in Australia. Also ensure that you have personal insurance or travel insurance with a comprehensive health component to cover the possibility of illness or accident.

Medicare, Australia's national health insurance, covers visitors from New Zealand, the UK, Ireland, Malta, Sweden, Italy, Finland, Norway, Belgium, Slovenia and the Netherlands. To be eligible, contact your national health programme before travelling to Australia to ensure that you have the correct documents should you need to enrol at a Medicare office (you can enrol before or after you receive treatment). The agreement provides urgent treatment but doesn't cover elective surgery, dental care, ambulance services or illness arising en route to Australia – in some cases it doesn't cover students from these countries studying in Australia. The agreements do not cover repatriation in the case of illness or injury. Such agreements are subject to change (check before you travel) and do not entirely replace travel insurance (make sure you're covered).

You are allowed to bring 'reasonable quantities' of prescribed, non-narcotic medications. All should be clearly labelled and identifiable. For large quantities, bring a doctor's certificate to produce to customs if necessary. All medication must be carried in personal hand luggage. Local chemists can fill most prescriptions – which must be written by an Australian-registered doctor.

Health hazards exist on the seas and in the countryside, starting with the threat of too much sun. High-factor sun-screen cream is essential, even on cloudy days.

Poisonous spiders live in Australia. The dark, bulbous, Sydney funnelweb is one of the world's most lethal and aggressive types of spider. Although its bites are rare (about 10 victims a year), they require immediate medical attention to stave off coma and death. Catch the spider (safely) for identification if you can. Other poisonous spiders include the redback, the eastern mouse spider and the white-tail.

Shark attacks are also rare, but one is too many. Swim between the flags and heed shark alarms.

In certain seasons and areas, the bluebottle **jellyfish** (also called Portuguese-man-of-war) may be encountered. Its sting is painful but can be treated. Far more dangerous are the box jellyfish (seawasp) and the similar irukandji, which are found in tropical waters from about October to April. A sting from either species can be fatal. Never disregard warning signs on beaches. In the north of Australia, **saltwater crocodiles** can be a menace to swimmers, especially in rivers and inland pools. Always obey warning signs. Other marine hazards include the stonefish and the blue-ringed octopus. Both can cause death.

Several of the world's deadliest **snakes**, including the brown snake, tiger snake, taipan and death adder, are indigenous to Australia. You are unlikely to encounter them in built-up areas. The inland taipan, or fierce snake, has the most potent venom in the world, but is restricted to sparsely populated areas of southwest Queensland, so few people are bitten. If you are bitten by any snake, seek immediate medical attention.

The good news is that you can drink water from taps anywhere unless specifically marked otherwise. In the Outback, warnings may read 'Bore water', 'Non-potable' or 'Not for drinking'.

M

MAPS

State and local tourist offices give away useful maps of their areas. If you need more detailed maps, check at newsstands and bookshops. Car hire companies often supply free city directories showing each street and place of interest. If you're driving beyond the cities you'll want to buy an up-to-date road map of the region. On the internet, see google maps and www.whereis.com.au

MEDIA

More than 500 newspapers are published in Australia, ranging from big-city dailies like the *Sydney Morning Herald* and *The Age* of Melbourne to small-circulation weeklies. Among the latter are local periodicals aimed at the various immigrant communities, published in Chinese, Dutch, French, German, Greek, Italian and other languages. In the bigger cities, specialist newsstands sell airmail copies of newspapers from London, Rome, New York and Paris, in addition to weekly and monthly American and European magazines. The UK *Guardian Weekly* is now printed in Sydney.

A specifically Australian version of the Guardian is now available on-line (www.theguardian.com/au).

ABC is the best TV station for quality content, while the commercial stations (7, 9 and 10) trot out game shows, reality TV and the occasional drama series. SBS (Special Broadcasting Service; www.sbs.com.au) is another excellent TV channel, servicing people with more eclectic and international tastes. SBS also has a range of radio and online media platforms catering for non-English speaking and specialist interest audiences. CNN and other satellite news services are available at most international-standard hotels.

MONEY

Australian currency is decimal, with the dollar the basic unit (100 cents to one dollar). Notes come in A$100, A$50, A$20, A$10 and A$5 denominations. Coins come in 5c, 10c, 20c, 50c, A$1 and A$2 denominations. There being no 1c or 2c coins, cash transactions are rounded up or down to the nearest 5c, so an item priced at A$11.99 will cost you A$12. Non-cash transactions, such as those using a credit card, are not subject to rounding.

All international airports in Australia provide **currency exchange** facilities, and foreign notes or travellers' cheques can be converted at most banks. Cash travellers' cheques at banks or larger hotels (despite the charges), as it is increasingly difficult elsewhere.

ATM machines are widespread. You should be able to obtain cash directly in this way using your credit/debit card and with the same PIN number you use at home.

N

NATIONAL PARKS

The vast majority of Australia's national parks are run by state- or territory-based authorities. Their details are as follows:

ACT: Parks and City Services; GPO 158 Canberra ACT 2601; tel: 13 22 81; www.environment.act.gov.au/parks-recreation

New South Wales: National Parks and Wildlife Service; tel: 1300 072 757; www.nationalparks.nsw.gov.au

Queensland: Queensland Department of National Parks, Recreation, Sport and Racing; tel: 13 74 68; www.nprsr.qld.gov.au

Northern Territory: Parks and Wildlife Service of Northern Territory; tel: 08-8999 4555; www.parksandwildlife.nt.gov.au

Western Australia: Department of Parks and Wildlife; tel: 08-9219 9000; www.dpaw.wa.gov.au

South Australia: National Parks South Australia 08-8204 1910; www.environment.sa.gov.au/parks

Victoria: Parks Victoria; tel: 13 19 63; www.parkweb.vic.gov.au

Tasmania: Parks and Wildlife Service Tasmania; tel: 1300 827 727; www.parks.tas.gov.au

A small number of parks, including Kakadu and Uluru–Kata Tjuta national parks, are managed by the federal government, under the auspices of the **Australian Department of Environment and Energy:** (www.environment.gov.au).

For information on the Great Barrier Reef Marine Park, contact the **Great Barrier Reef Marine Park Authority** (www.gbrmpa.gov.au).

O

OPENING HOURS

Banks generally open Monday to Thursday from 9.30am to 4pm and Friday 9.30am to 5pm. In the big cities, selected banking facilities may be available on Saturday morning, but don't rely on it.

General **office hours** are Monday to Friday 9am to 5pm.

Shopping: Most shops close at 5 or 5.30pm on weekdays. In most towns, shops have one (or sometimes two) late shopping nights a week, when stores stay open to 9 or 9.30 pm. This is usually on Thursday or Friday. Sunday trading is quite common in larger cities and suburban malls.

Bars, pubs and hotels: Licensing hours vary by state, but a typical schedule would be Monday to Saturday 10am–11pm or midnight (often later Friday and Saturday), with most pubs open by noon on Sundays as well, closing at 10 or 11pm.

P

POLICE

Each state operates its own police force, covering urban and rural areas. The federal police force has jurisdiction over government property, including airports. The police emergency phone number is 000.

POST OFFICES

Australia's post offices are signposted 'Australia Post'. Most branches adhere to a 9am–5pm schedule Monday to Friday, though big-city General Post Offices often remain open for extended hours.

Postcards and letters to the UK, US or Europe cost A$2.75, and international aerograms cost A$2.40, whatever their destination. Local letters cost from A$1. Mailboxes throughout Australia are red, with an Australia Post logo.

PUBLIC HOLIDAYS

1 January New Year's Day
26 January Australia Day
25 April Anzac Day
25 December Christmas Day
26 December Boxing Day
Moveable dates Good Friday, Easter, Easter Monday, Queen's Birthday

Additional public holidays are celebrated only in certain states, while other holidays are observed at different times in different states. School holidays arrive four times a year; the longest one is in the summer through the latter part of December and all of January, tending to crowd hotels and tourist attractions.

R

RELIGION

The major religion in Australia is Christianity. Of the non-Christian faiths, Buddhists are the largest group, followed by Muslims, Hindus and Jews. To find the place of worship of your choice, look on the Yellow Pages website under 'Churches and Synagogues'.

T

TAX REFUNDS

A Goods and Services Tax (GST) of 10 percent applies to most purchases. The Tourist Refund Scheme (TRS) allows overseas visitors to claim a limited GST refund as they clear customs. To qualify for the TRS you need to have spent at least A$300 (including GST), either from the same store (at the one time or over several occasions – but a single tax invoice for all the goods must be provided), or from several stores, no more than 30 days before you leave Australia. You must also take the goods with you as carry-on luggage.

TELEPHONES

Australia's country code is 61. This is followed by a city code (2 for NSW or the ACT, 3 for Victoria and Tasmania, 7 for Queensland and 8 for the Northern Territory, South Australia and Western Australia).

You can dial anywhere in the country from almost any land line, even in the Outback, and expect a loud and clear line. Many hotel rooms have phones from which you can dial cross-Australia (STD) or internationally (IDD). Some hotels add a surcharge to your telephone bill.

The minimum cost of a local public payphone call is 50c. Long-distance calls within Australia (STD) and International Direct Dialing (IDD) calls can be made on public payphones. Check with the operator for these charges as they vary for distances and the time of day of the call. Public payphones accept most coins and Phonecards. A Phonecard is a pre-paid card for use in public payphones to make local, STD and IDD calls. Phonecards are sold at newsagents, post offices and other shops. The Telstra PhoneAway card enables you to use virtually any phone in Australia – home and office phones, mobile phones, hotel and payphones – all call costs are charged against the card.

Creditphones accept most major credit cards such as Amex, Visa and MasterCard and can be found at international and domestic airports, and many hotels. To make a reverse-charge (collect) call, phone the International Operator, tel: 1225.

Australia's digital mobile (cell) phone network is dominated by 3G UMTS 2100 and is compatible with 2G GSM 900 and 1800 European phones. It is easy to buy pre-paid sim cards (and cheap phones) from suppliers such as Telstra (www.telstra.com.au) and Optus (www.optus.com.au). Mobile phone retail outlets abound in all cities.

Telephone directories give instructions on dialling and details on emergency and other services. To reach an overseas number, dial 0011, then the country code of the destination, the area code and the local number.

TIME ZONES

Australia has three time zones: Eastern Standard Time (EST), which operates in New South Wales, Australian Capital Territory, Victoria, Tasmania and Queensland; Central Standard Time (CST) in South Australia and Northern Territory (and in the NSW Outback town of Broken Hill); and Western Standard Time (WST) in Western Australia.

CST is 30 minutes behind EST, while WST is two hours behind EST. Daylight saving (setting the clocks forward an hour) operates in all states and territories, except Queensland and the Northern Territory, from the beginning of October through to the first week in April.

Sydney is on EST, which is 10 hours ahead of Greenwich Mean Time and 15 hours ahead of New York. Time differences between Australia's zones and other countries vary seasonally as daylight saving is switched on and off by Australia or the other country. So when it's winter in the northern hemisphere, and daylight saving is operating in New South Wales, the time difference between London and Sydney is 11 hours. But during British Summertime, when Sydney is on EST, it's only nine hours. One way to get it right is to access www.timeanddate.com/worldclock and use the calculator.

TIPPING

Tipping is discretionary, and nobody's livelihood depends on it. It is not customary to tip taxi drivers, porters at airports or hairdressers, although you may do so if you wish. Porters have set charges at railway terminals, but not at hotels. Hotels and restaurants do not usually add service charges to accounts, although some restaurants and cafés add a 10 percent surcharge for service on public holidays. In restaurants, patrons usually tip food and drink waiters up to 10 percent, but only if service is good. (If you are ecstatic about the service, make it 15 percent.) If service is poor or a waiter is surly or impolite, don't tip.

TOILETS

'Dunny' is the Aussie slang term for toilet, but 'washroom', 'restrooms', 'loos', 'ladies' or 'gents' are all understood. Public toilets are often locked after certain hours, but you can generally use the facilities in any pub or cinema complex without needing to buy a drink or a movie ticket, and department store toilets are always handy.

TOURIST INFORMATION

To obtain tourist information before you leave home, access the website of Tourism Australia www.tourism.australia.com or contact them in your country of residence or at their Australian head office:
Level 29, 420 George Street, Sydney NSW 2000, Australia; tel: 02-9360 1111.

Overseas Tourism Australia offices:
UK: Australia Centre, Australia House, 6th Floor, Melbourne Place, The Strand, London WC2B 4LG; tel: (020) 7438 4600.
US: 2029 Century Park, E Ste 3150, Los Angeles CA 90067; tel: (310) 695 3200.
New Zealand: General Manager Jenny Aitken; jaitken@tourism.australia.com; tel: (09) 377 0448.

State tourist offices in Australia are:
Canberra and Region Visitors Centre: Regatta Point, Barrine Drive, Parkes, ACT 2600; tel: 1300 554 114.
Sydney Visitor Centre: Corner Argyle and Playfair streets, The Rocks, Sydney NSW 2000; tel: 1800 067 676 or 02-9240 8788.

Tourism Top End: 6 Bennett Street (Corner Bennett and Smith Streets), Darwin NT 0800; tel: 1300 138 886 or 08-8980 6000.

South Australia Visitors Centre: James Place (off Rundle Mall), Adelaide SA 5000; tel: 1300-655 276.

Melbourne Visitor Centre: Federation Square, Corner Swanston and Flinders Streets, Melbourne; tel: 03-9655 1900.

Western Australian Visitor Centre: 55 William Street, Perth, WA 6000; tel: 1800 812 808.

Even in the smallest town you will find an outlet distributing local tourist information and advice. Look for the ubiquitous 'i' sign.

TRANSPORT

Public transport is highly developed in most Australian cities, although each state has its own privatisation arrangement and ticketing system. For timetable information in NSW and Sydney, including buses, trains and ferries, see www.transportnsw.info. Note that Sydney Airport is connected directly to the city by rail. A fine fleet of ferries is concentrated at Circular Quay. The ferries provide cheap outings for sightseers to Manly, Watsons Bay, Cremorne Point, Neutral Bay or Taronga Zoo. A combination ticket for the ferry and zoo entry is available for purchase at the ferry terminal for a small discount.

For information on Victoria and Melbourne's train, tram and bus networks see http://ptv.vic.gov.au. Melbourne's trams are not only decorative – they're a vital part of city transport. The gold-and-burgundy-coloured City Circle tram is free.

In Adelaide (www.adelaidemetro.com.au), trams run to Glenelg, and the O-Bahn ('bullet bus') provides highly efficient transport to outer suburbs.

For information on train and bus connections in Brisbane and Queensland see www.translink.com.au; Perth and Western Australia see www.pta.wa.gov.au, the Northern Territory see www.transport.nt.gov.au/public; Hobart and Tasmania see www.metrotas.com.au.

V

VISAS AND ENTRY REQUIREMENTS

Australia requires all visitors to hold a visa. The visa you need depends on what your visit is for and how long you plan to stay. Citizens of New Zealand (which has close links with Australia) receive an automatic electronic visa when they present their passports at the Immigration desk.

Most European passport holders are eligible for an eVisitor visa (or Electronic Travel Authority), which is free and can be obtained online at www.border.gov.au, the website of the Department of Immigration and Border Protection. These electronic visas (there's no stamp in your passport) usually last 12 months and are valid for visits of no more than three months' duration. Return visits within the 12-month period are allowed.

The Electronic Travel Authority (ETA) allows travel agents and airlines to issue a visa electronically to visitors at the time of flight booking in their home countries. You can also apply yourself online at www.eta.immi.gov.au. People visiting friends or relatives or just coming as tourists should apply for the Visitor ETA, which costs A$20. It entitles you to stays of up to three months in Australia within 12 months of the ETA's issue.

If you wish to extend your stay beyond three months, you will need to apply to the department for a Tourist Visa. See the department's website for details.

If you are not a passport holder of one of the eVisitor- or ETA-approved countries, or plan to stay longer than three months, you should apply for a Tourist Visa, valid for up to 12 months. You can download a visa application form from the department's website. An application fee is payable.

Australia operates reciprocal working holiday programmes with countries including Belgium, Canada, Cyprus, Denmark, Estonia, Finland, France, Germany, Hong Kong, Ireland, Italy, Japan, Korea, Malta, the Netherlands, Norway, Sweden, Taiwan and the UK, for applicants between 18 and 30, either single or married without children. Working holiday visas allow recipients to live and work in Australia for up to one year (sometimes longer if they work in a rural area for a period – check for updates).

On arrival in Australia, you may have to show your return or onward ticket, and prove that you have sufficient funds for your stay. On entry, each person may take into Australia duty-free up to 2.25 litres (about 0.5 gallon) of alcohol and 250 cigarettes or 250g (9oz) of tobacco. Internet cafés exist in all Australian cities and most towns.

W

WEBSITES AND INTERNET ACCESS

Tourism and travel
Tourism Australia: www.tourism.australia.com
Travel Online: www.travelonline.com
Australian Travel and Tourism: www.atn.com.au
Western Australian Tourism: www.westernaustralia.com
Northern Territory Tourist Commission: http://en.travelnt.com
Tourism Tasmania: www.discovertasmania.com.au
Tourism Victoria: www.visitvictoria.com
Tourism New South Wales: www.visitnsw.com.au
South Australian Tourist Commission: www.southaustralia.com
Tourism Queensland: www.queenslandholidays.com
Tropical North Queensland: www.ttnq.org.au
Canberra Tourism: www.visitcanberra.com.au
Information and services
Visas: www.border.gov.au or www.eta.immi.gov.au
Latest currency exchange rates: www.xe.com
Department of Environment and Energy: www.environment.gov.au
Media
Australian Broadcasting Corporation: www.abc.net.au

Special Broadcasting Service: www.sbs.com.au
Sydney Morning Herald: www.smh.com.au
Melbourne Age: www.theage.com.au
Internet cafés and subscription Wi-fi exist in all Australian cities and most towns. Free Wi-fi is increasingly common in cafés, pubs, restaurants, shops and travel hubs.

YOUTH HOSTELS

There are two types of hostel accommodation: privately owned backpacker hostels and YHA (Youth Hostels Association) Hostels. Both provide self-catering accommodation from about A$35 a night.

The Australian YHA is Australia's largest budget accommodation network, with more than 140 hostels in a wide range of locations. They are open to all ages and offer sleeping, self-catering kitchens and common rooms where you'll meet fellow travellers.

You can join the YHA in your own country or in Australia. Contact the YHA (3/9 Castlereagh Street, Sydney, NSW 2000; tel: 02-9261 1111; www.yha.com.au) for a free information pack giving membership details and a list of hostels.

INDEX

Adelaide 145
  Adelaide Festival
    Centre 148
  Adelaide Skycity 149
  Art Gallery of South
    Australia 149
  Ayers House 150
  Botanic Gardens 150
  Central Market 147
  Government House
    149
  Holy Trinity Church
    150
  Migration Museum
    149
  North Terrace 148
  Parliament House
    148
  Rundle Mall 150
  South Australian
    Museum 149
  Tandanya 151
Adelaide Hills 152
Airlie Beach, QLD 100
Alice Springs Desert
  Park, NT 116
Alice Springs, NT 113
Apollo Bay, VIC 180
Australia Zoo QLD 89
Avon Valley, WA 136
Ayers Rock (Uluru),
  NT 117

Ballarat, VIC 30, 177
  Botanical Gardens
    178

Barossa Valley, SA 153
Bedarra Island, QLD 97
Bells Beach, VIC 180
Bendigo, VIC 178
Blackheath, NSW 64
Blue Mountains, NSW 63
Bourke, NSW 70
Brampton Island,
  QLD 93
Brisbane 80, 81
  Botanic Gardens 82
  Chinatown 84
  King George Square
    82
  Old Windmill 81
  Parliament House 82
  Queensland Cultural
    Centre 83
  Queen Street Mall 82
  South Bank 82
Broken Hill, NSW 70
Broome, WA 144
Byron Bay, NSW 67

Caloundra, QLD 89
Canberra 71
  Aboriginal Tent
    Embassy 77
  Australian war
    Memorial 75
  Black Mountain
    Tower 74
  Botanic Gardens 74
  Canberra Deep Space
    Communication
    Complex, ACT 79

  Civic Centre 74
  National Botanic
    Gardens 74
  National Carillon 74
  National Gallery of
    Australia 75
  National Museum of
    Australia 74
  National Portrait
    Gallery 76
  National Zoo and
    Aquarium 78
  Old Parliament
    House 77
  Parliament House
    78
  Questacon 77
  Regatta Point 73
  Royal Australian
    Mint 78
Cape Tribulation, QLD
  102
Cape York Peninsula,
  QLD 103
Cataract Gorge,
  Launceston 190
Ceduna, SA 158
Cessnock, NSW 66
Coober Pedy, SA 159
Cooktown, QLD 91, 103
Coolgardie, WA 141
Cradle Mountain-Lake St
  Clair National Park,
  TAS 191
Currumbin Wildlife
  Sanctuary, QLD 87

Daintree National Park, QLD 102
Dandenong Ranges, VIC 173
Darling Range, WA 136
Darwin 104
    Aquascene 108
    Chinese Temple 107
    Crocodylus Park 108
    Darwin Waterfront 107
    Fannie Bay Gaol Museum 106
    Government House 106
    Indo-Pacific Marine Exhibition 107
    Mindil Beach Sunset Markets 105
    Museum and Art Gallery of the Northern Territory 107
    Parliament House 106
    SkyCity Darwin 107
Daydream Island, QLD 95
Dubbo, NSW 69

Eungella National Park, QLD 99
Eyre Peninsula, SA 157

Fitzroy Island, QLD 97
Flagstaff Hill Maritime Museum, VIC 181
Fleurieu Peninsula, SA 156
Flinders Chase National Park, SA 156
Flinders Ranges, SA 158

Flying Doctor Service 114
Fogg Dam Conservation Reserve, NT 109
Fraser Island, QLD 92
Fremantle, WA 132
    Fremantle Arts Centre 135
    Monument Hill 133
    Old Fremantle Prison 134
    Round House 134
    Western Australian Maritime Museum 134
Freshwater Bay, WA 132

Geraldton, WA 137
Glenelg, Adelaide 151
Gold Coast, QLD 85
Great Barrier Reef, QLD 90
Great Keppel Island, QLD 93
Great Ocean Road, VIC 179
Great Otway National Park, VIC 180
Green Island, QLD 98

Hahndorf, SA 152
Hayman Island, QLD 96
Healesville Sanctuary, VIC 174
Healesville, VIC 174
Heron Island, QLD 93
Hinchinbrook Island, QLD 96
Hobart 184
    Battery Point 185
    Constitution Dock 185

Maritime Museum of Tasmania 186
Narryna Heritage Museum 185
Parliament House 185
Salamanca Place 185
Shot Tower 186
Tasmanian Museum and Art Gallery 186
Hunter Valley, NSW 66

James Boag,Brewery Experience Launceston 190
Jenolan Caves, NSW 65
Jervis Bay, ACT 68
Jumping Crocodile Cruise, NT 109

Kakadu National Park, NT 109
Kalgoorlie, WA 140
Kangaroo Island, SA 154
Kata Tjuta (Olgas), NT 119
Katherine Gorge, NT 111
Katoomba, NSW 64
Kings Canyon, NT 117
Kingscote, SA 156
Kingston, TAS 187
Kosciuszko National Park, NSW 69
Kuranda, QLD 101
Ku-ring-gai Chase National Park, NSW 65

Lady Elliot Island, QLD 92
Lake Burley Griffin, Canberra 73

Launceston, TAS 189
    Design Centre 189
    Macquarie House 189
Leeuwin-Naturaliste
    National Park, WA 139
Lightning Ridge, NSW 70
Lincoln National Park,
    SA 157
Lindeman Island, QLD 94
Litchfield National Park,
    NT 108
Lizard Island, QLD 98
Lone Pine Koala
    Sanctuary, QLD 85
Long Island, QLD 95
Lord Howe Island,
    NSW 67

Mackay, QLD 99
Magnetic Island, QLD 96
Margaret River, WA 139
Maslins Beach, SA 157
McLaren Vale, SA 157
Melbourne 161
    Block Arcade 168
    Botanic Gardens 170
    Bourke Street Mall
        168
    Captain Cook's
        Cottage 169
    Carlton 171
    Chinatown 169
    Crown Entertainment
        Complex 164
    Eureka Skydeck88 164
    Federation Square
        167
    Fitzroy 172
    Government House
        171

Hamer Hall 166
Ian Potter Centre:
    NGV Australia 167
La Trobe's Cottage
    171
Medibank Icehouse
    165
Melbourne Docklands
    165
Melbourne Museum
    169
Melbourne Star 165
Melbourne Zoo 171
NGV International 165
Old Melbourne Gaol
    169
Parliament House 168
Queen Victoria Market
    170, 212
Shrine of
    Remembrance 171
Southbank 164
South Yarra 172
St Kilda 172
St Paul's Cathedral
    166
Theatres Building 166
Toorak 172
Victorian Arts Centre
    165
Mornington Peninsula,
    VIC 174
Mossman, QLD 103
Mt Coot-tha Botanic
    Gardens, QLD 84
Mt Wellington, Hobart
    184
Murray River, SA 152
Museum of Central
    Australia, NT 116

Nambour, QLD 89
Newcastle, NSW 66
Ngilgi Caves, WA 139
Noosa, QLD 89
Nullarbor Plain, SA 158

Old Mill, WA 132
Olgas (Kata Tjuta), NT
    119
Orpheus Island, QLD 96

Perisher Valley, NSW 69
Perth 127
    Aquarium of Western
        Australia 131
    Art Gallery of Western
        Australia 131
    Barracks Archway 130
    Government House
        130
    Hay Street Mall 130
    King's Park 128
    Northbridge 131
    Old Courthouse 129
    Parliament House 131
    Perth Institute of
        Contemporary
        Arts 131
    Stirling Gardens 129
    Swan Bells Tower 129
    Swan River 128
    Western Australia
        Museum 130
Phillip Island, VIC 175
Pinnacles Desert, WA 138
Port Arthur, TAS 187
Port Campbell National
    Park, VIC 181
Port Douglas, QLD 102
Port Fairy, VIC 181

Port Lincoln, SA 157
Port Stephens, NSW 67
Proserpine, QLD 100

Reef HQ 91, 100
Rockhampton, QLD 98
Rottnest Island, WA 135

Seal Bay, SA 156
Sherbrooke Forest Park, VIC 173
Shipwreck Coast, VIC 180
Shute Harbour, QLD 95, 100
Snowy Mountains, NSW 68
South Molle Island, QLD 95
South West National Park, TAS 191
Sovereign Hill, VIC 178
Standley Chasm, NT 116
Sunshine Coast, QLD 88
Surfers Paradise, QLD 87
Swan Valley, WA 136
Sydney 40
    Anzac War Memorial 52
    Argyle Cut 45
    Art Gallery of NSW 54
    Australian Museum 53
    Bondi beach 62
    Botanic Gardens 55
    Cadman's Cottage 44
    Centennial Park 55
    Chinatown 50
    Cockle Bay 51
    Cook and Phillip Park 52

Darling Harbour 51
Dawes Point Park 47
Domain 54
Elizabeth Bay House 57
Fort Denison 59
Holy Trinity Church 46
Hyde Park 52
Hyde Park Barracks 54
Kings Cross 56
King Street Wharf 51
Manly 61
Martin Place 49
Mrs Macquarie's Point 55
Museum of Contemporary Art 44
Museum of Sydney 45
National Maritime Museum 52
Observatory Hill 47
Olympic Park 62
Paddington 55, 57
Paddy's Market 50, 212
Port Jackson 40
Queen Victoria Building 49, 207
Rocks, The 43
St Andrew's 50
St Mary's Cathedral 52
Sydney Aquarium 51
Sydney Harbour Bridge 47
Sydney Observatory 47

Sydney Opera House 42, 204
Sydney Tower 48
Sydney Wildlife World 51
Taronga Zoo 59
Vaucluse House 60
Watsons Bay 60

Taroona, TAS 186
The Kimberley, WA 142
Thredbo, NSW 69
Three Sisters, NSW 64
Tidbinbilla Nature Reserve, ACT 79
Tjapukai Aboriginal Cultural Park, QLD 102
Townsville, QLD 100

Uluru (Ayers Rock), NT 117

Victor Harbor, SA 156

Wave Rock, WA 138
Whyalla, SA 157
William Ricketts Sanctuary, VIC 173
Wilpena Pound, SA 159
Wilsons Promontory, VIC 177
Wolfe Creek Meteorite National Park, WA 143

Yanchep National Park, WA 137
Yarra Valley, VIC 174
Yorke Peninsula, SA 157
Yulara, NT 117, 121

INSIGHT ⊙ GUIDES POCKET GUIDE

AUSTRALIA

First Edition 2017

Editor: Sian Marsh
Author: Ken Bernstein, Lindsay Brown,
Malgorzata Anczewska
Head of Production: Rebeka Davies
Picture Editor: Tom Smyth
Cartography Update: Carte
Update Production: Apa Digital
Photography Credits: 123RF 5MC, 11, 29;
Australian Capital Tourism 32, 75; AWL
Images 38; Bigstock 199; Dreamstime 5M,
5TC, 36, 45, 52, 64, 113, 119, 129, 144, 150,
179, 187, 203; Getty Images 1, 4TC, 4ML,
13, 16, 22, 40, 104, 192, 204; Glyn Genin/Apa
Publications 5M, 6L, 23, 43, 44, 46, 48, 50,
53, 54, 56, 59, 61, 106, 108, 109, 110, 112,
115, 116, 120, 123, 127, 130, 147, 154, 208,
220, 223; Hamilton Lund/Tourism NSW 41,
51; iStock 4TL, 5T, 5MC, 14, 25, 57, 58, 62,
65, 67, 71, 76, 92, 97, 99, 133, 134, 138, 140,
153, 160, 174, 176, 178, 182, 191, 215; Jerry
Dennis/Apa Publications 34, 172, 219; Jon
Davison/Apa Publications 30, 156; Kuranda
Scenic Railway 101; Peter Stuckings/Apa
Publications 18, 79, 81, 82, 83, 84, 86, 88, 89,
94, 100, 103, 210, 212; Pro Dive Cairns 4MC,
7R, 90, 195; Public domain 26; Shutterstock
180; Steven Greaves/APA Publications 196;
Tourism Australia 7, 21, 87, 121, 125, 137,
142, 149, 158; Tourism NSW 66, 69; Virginia
Star/Apa Publications 6R, 163, 164, 166, 168,
170, 200, 206, 217
Cover Picture: Shutterstock

Distribution
UK, Ireland and Europe: Apa Publications
(UK) Ltd; sales@insightguides.com
United States and Canada: Ingram
Publisher Services; ips@ingramcontent.com
Australia and New Zealand: Woodslane;
info@woodslane.com.au
Southeast Asia: Apa Publications (SN) Pte;
singaporeoffice@insightguides.com
Hong Kong, Taiwan and China:
Apa Publications (HK) Ltd;
hongkongoffice@insightguides.com
Worldwide: Apa Publications (UK) Ltd;
sales@insightguides.com

**Special Sales, Content Licensing
and CoPublishing**
Insight Guides can be purchased in bulk
quantities at discounted prices. We can
create special editions, personalised jackets
and corporate imprints tailored to your
needs. sales@insightguides.com;
www.insightguides.biz

All Rights Reserved
© 2017 Apa Digital (CH) AG and
Apa Publications (UK) Ltd

Printed in China by CTPS

No part of this book may be reproduced,
stored in a retrieval system or transmitted in
any form or means electronic, mechanical,
photocopying, recording or otherwise,
without prior written permission from Apa
Publications.

Contact us
Every effort has been made to provide
accurate information in this publication,
but changes are inevitable. The publisher
cannot be responsible for any resulting loss,
inconvenience or injury. We would appreciate
it if readers would call our attention to any
errors or outdated information. We also
welcome your suggestions; please contact
us at: hello@insightguides.com
www.insightguides.com

SIGHT ⊙ GUIDES

FF THE SHELF

e 1970, **INSIGHT GUIDES** has provided a unique perspective on world's best travel destinations by using specially commissioned ography and illuminating text written by local authors.

her you're planning a city break, a walking tour or the journey of a lifetime, uperb range of guidebooks and phrasebooks will inspire you to discover about your chosen destination.

GHT GUIDES

a unique combination of stunning photos, ioing narrative and detailed maps, providing inspiration and information you need.

PHRASEBOOKS & DICTIONARIES

help users to feel at home, when away. Pocket-sized with a free app to download, they go where you do.

GUIDES

iundreds of great photos into a smaller t with detailed practical information, so you vigate the world's top cities with confidence.

EXPLORE GUIDES

feature easy-to-follow walks and itineraries in the world's most exciting destinations, with our choice of the best places to eat and drink along the way.

KET GUIDES

ne concise information on where to go and to do in a handy compact format, ideal on ound. Includes a full-colour, fold-out map.

EXPERIENCE GUIDES

feature offbeat perspectives and secret gems for experienced travellers, with a collection of over 100 ideas for a memorable stay in a city.

www.insightguides.com